Stepping Into You

*The Blueprint to Nail Your
Personal Brand and
Market Yourself Magnificently*

Gwyneth Letherbarrow

www.feelgoodcoachingandconsulting.com

ISBN-13: 978-3200055506 (Feelgood Coaching and Consulting e.U.)
ISBN-10: 3200055502

DEDICATION

This book is dedicated to the fabulous being inside of you, just waiting to light up and sparkle, and step into the spotlight.

Table of Contents

INTRODUCTION

"You'll never make anything of yourself if you don't go to College".

Those angry words came from my Grandad in the summer of 1981, just a few weeks before my 16th birthday.

As I completed the last of my exams at secondary school, I suddenly woke up to the fact that there were no laws which could force me to continue to college. It wasn't who I was. I had hated school for 12 years, so what was the point of prolonging the pain. Instead I wanted to work for the United Nations and save the world.

My Grandad was furious. He began by offering me money to continue to study, then he shouted at me for being stupid. After that we avoided speaking to each other for almost a year.

I learned very quickly that neither I, nor the United Nations, could save the world, but it was the beginning of a career spanning 20 years, working in the public and private sectors, helping others to help themselves. And I loved it.

Following my gut, aligning my values and passions with my work was one of the best things I ever did. I created my very own personal brand, and encouraged those I worked with to do the same by aligning with their objectives and purpose, and being true to themselves.

This book is the result of everything I experienced and learned, and is going to show you how to find *your* personal brand, so that by the time you have finished reading you will feel comfortable about marketing and promoting yourself to others, allowing you to own your authenticity and brilliance.

Why personal branding?

In an age when a large percentage of businesses are using social media to promote their services and products, the modern entrepreneur already has a personal brand, whether they want one or not.

The importance of managing personal branding and image is highlighted in an article by Ryan Erskine ('22 Statistics that Prove the Value of Personal Branding', www.ryanerskine.com). Erskine states that 'reputation damage is the #1 risk concern for business executives around the world'.

That research also shows that out of the total number of users looking to the internet to research people and companies, 65 per cent believe that online information is a trustworthy resource, and more than 50 per cent of users have discounted a vendor or contractor based on what they found.

Within my own business, the number one complaint/problem that my clients bring to me is that they do not feel comfortable talking about themselves with other humans, let alone presenting themselves to the world via social media.

They lack confidence when marketing their business online and offline, and having to pitch their business to a bank or venture capitalist for funding sometimes triggers pure panic.

For you as a female entrepreneur, that can mean that at a minimum you fail to reach your full potential, and the worst-case scenario is that your business collapses.

Although there are no official statistics on this issue – indeed the report produced by Barclays Bank in March 2017 (www.home.barclays/news) identified data collection on female entrepreneurship as lacking – additional research supports the idea that one of the greatest concerns that women in business have is that they will come across as being aggressive and that promoting themselves and their business goes against social expectations (i.e. they feel uncomfortable talking about their achievements).

In addition to not fitting in, there is also a lot of fear about not being clever enough to be successful and wealthy or not having academic qualifications. I see so many women comparing themselves to others and deciding that they simply aren't good enough to do what they want to do. I see so many women branding themselves as tired and hopeless human beings.

And despite huge progress during recent years, there are still a lot of people who judge women for wanting to have a job *and* a family. If a woman decides to stay at home with her children, getting back into the job market or business can seem an insurmountable challenge. And if they put their career first, they're frequently told that they're a bad Mother.

If you're here, I know that you're at least willing to test the waters to see whether you've got what it takes to define and align with your personal brand and then create the future of your dreams.

I'm not asking you to make massive changes all at once, and I am not coming from the 'men against women' perspective. I believe in 'live and let live'. I believe that we are all unique and at the same time equal.

How to use this book

As you're going through this book, please be honest with yourself about what you want, and why you haven't got it yet (what is holding you back from having it?).

The blueprint in this book is split into five parts.

We begin with ALIGN which takes you back to basics, looking at your core values and showing you how to clean off that dust you've allowed to cover your fabulous personality – because you have to change what's happening on the inside before you can start changing what's happening on the outside.

You'll then move on to RELEASE where I'm going to set you some challenges to help you decide what you want to keep in your life and what has to go. Letting go of old habits and beliefs can be difficult, so you'll find plenty of tools to make the changes more manageable.

The third element of the Blueprint is TRUST, aimed at helping you to begin trusting your personal brand, to effectively deal with judgement and criticism, and to learn how to depend on your own feedback.

Part four is TRANSFORM where I introduce you to the practical work of building your personal brand. You'll begin to develop a strategy for networking, online and offline, and you'll learn about the power of video. You'll also find a description of the major social media platforms which will help you to choose which of them require your presence.

The final part of the Blueprint is THRIVE where you're going to pull everything together and take action. You'll find tools and advice that will help you put together a business presentation, as well as ideas about how to keep your personal brand steady – until of course you want to start reinventing yourself all over again.

There are templates and worksheets for you to download as you work through the activities. Some will take longer than others. You can access them all here: **http://bit.ly/SIY_The_Downloads**

If you choose to download all the templates in one session then that's fine, but the Blueprint is structured to allow you to build and market your brand without you getting into a panic about what you need to do. I would therefore urge you to download the relevant information only when you read about it.

This would be a great time to purchase yourself an A4 binder to keep all your notes, activities and ideas in one place because as you move through the book you will see that the downloadable templates and other tools contribute to your personal branding content library and strategy.

What you will learn in these pages will get you the results that you desire, but only if you are willing to take full ownership for your future and do the necessary work.

A part of my work ethos is to focus on a win/win outcome, and it's because I am passionate about *you succeeding* that I want you to be able to present the most fabulous version of yourself to the business world.

So there's just one more thing you need to do before you turn the page, and that is to commit to yourself, because a big reason for failure in the world is because we plan too much and take too little action.

Although it's not essential, if you know that you're the type of person who thinks that they simply don't have enough hours in a day to do everything they want to, you will find my time management tool very useful, and you can download it at **http://bit.ly/SIY_The_Downloads**

Get clear on your outcomes for all your activities, set your intentions, and put time in your diary to build the brand that is you. I'll be cheering you on every step of the way. Be fabulous.

Let's do this !

Part One

ALIGN

Chapter 1 ~ The Voice of Un-Reason

"A belief is nothing more than a chronic pattern of thought" –
Esther Hicks

Every client I have ever worked with has started off by giving me a
long list of reasons about why they are no good at promoting or
marketing themselves.

They feel egotistical, they feel sleazy and yucky, they're worried
that others will make fun of them; they don't feel comfortable
with highlighting their skills, strengths and achievements because
they don't believe that they have something special to offer.

By the end of this chapter you are going to have learned how I
have helped those clients turn those negative beliefs around so
that you can do it too.

The psychology and the science

As a coach, it isn't my job to ask you to analyse and dissect your
past, and anyway, none of us can go back and make things

different. But to understand the 'why' behind all those doubts, I want to describe to you a common childhood scenario.

Growing up you were probably told to keep the noise down if you were playing too loudly, and at school your teacher will have told you to be quiet in the classroom. Then as a teenager you may have been accused of being rowdy or disruptive whilst you were enjoying some time with your friends.

When you first started a new job it's likely that you made a great effort to fit in so that you were liked by everybody, and that meant smiling and nodding and not causing trouble.

We were all encouraged keep the peace, conform to expectations, and if we didn't, we were considered to be rude and rebellious. And that's a short summary of why you don't enjoy talking about yourself today. The majority of people I speak to have been keeping quiet and not talking about themselves for decades.

So having briefly looked at the psychological aspect, it's useful to take this from the perspective of neuro-science (because being a Virgo I just love to combine the intangible with hard evidence) and introduce you to something called the 'reticular activating system' or 'RAS'.

The RAS is a group of cells that sits at the stem of our brains and affects our perception of everything (www.joecasanova.com). A brilliant example of what the RAS can do and how willing we are to do what we're told is demonstrated with an experiment conducted at Harvard University by Christopher Chabris and Daniel Simons.

They asked a small audience of people to watch a basketball game on video, where one team wore white t-shirts, and the other black. The audience was then told to count the number of times the white team passed the ball.

During the game, a person in a gorilla costume strolled onto the court, faced the camera and spent some nine seconds on screen.

Yet when asked after the game was finished, only half of those watching had seen the gorilla. The other half had been completely focused on keeping count of the number of times that the ball had been passed, as they had been instructed to do, and hadn't seen anything strange.

The audience hadn't expected to see anything different than a basketball game, and their brains programmed themselves accordingly.

If you are someone who has always done what they are told and are quite happy with your life, then you are likely to do what you believe others expect of you.

In the same way, and as was demonstrated in the gorilla experiment, it doesn't usually occur to us to question so-called professionals or experts (doctors, lawyers, accountants, professors) because we have assumed from a young age that they know what they're talking about, and we willingly follow their instructions.

As already mentioned, such behaviour stems from beliefs that you acquired when you were growing up. Every time your parents told you to 'be quiet' or 'go and do your homework' as a child, you will have combined that instruction with the emotion of being told what to do by someone with authority, and your RAS allowed those comments up into your conscious.

With frequent repetition, such instructions caused the relevant neural pathways to become more pronounced. You accepted and believed what you were told. You didn't speak at the meal table and you knew that doing your homework didn't involve making a choice.

Whilst the realisation that you have inadvertently given up some of your free will may create discomfort, with an increased understanding of the power of the RAS, science has proved that you CAN create new neural pathways (thoughts) IF you want to – and put aside beliefs that no longer serve you - which means you have the potential to create a completely different reality for yourself.

Obliterate the imposter syndrome

The term 'Imposter Syndrome' was first defined in 1978 by clinical psychologists Dr. Pauline R. Clance and Suzanne A. Imes, and refers to individuals who fail to reach their full potential because they fear that they will be exposed as being a fraud. They put any success down to being a fluke, or luck, and are unwilling to acknowledge that their achievements are a direct result of their own abilities.

It is frighteningly common (according to 'Frontiers in Psychology' around 70 per cent of us, men and women alike, experience the imposter syndrome at some degree or another) and in extreme cases it can lead to mental health problems, so it's important that you address it.

*How Does That Little Voice Inside Your Head Get There***?**

Depending upon which scientist you choose to believe, we have between 50,000 and 80,000 thoughts each day.   I like what Deepak Chopra says on the subject because he uses language that most people can understand, and puts the importance of that statistic into perspective.

"We each have an estimated 60,000 to 80,000 thoughts a day – unfortunately, many of them are the same thoughts we had yesterday, last week, and last year. The mind tends to get stuck in repetitive thought loops that squeeze out the possibility for new ideas and inspiration."   ("Why Meditate?" Blog/Article dated 5 March 2017 on www.deepakchopra.com).

The research shows that approximately two-thirds of those thousands of repetitive thoughts are things such as "I don't like any of my clothes and don't know what to wear today", or "I must remember to buy milk/bread/coffee" … and approximately two-thirds of *those* repetitive thoughts are negative, such as "I don't know when I'm supposed to do the shopping because I have a thousand other things to do", or "I desperately need a haircut" or "I'm going to be late for my appointment" – and so on.

Then the comparisons begin and your ego suffers. You tell yourself that no-one will ever want to work with you, you wonder how other women have succeeded and conclude that they had great connections or loads of help, things that you'll never have, and before you know it you're on a train to nowhere.
But where is the evidence of others being more clever or better organised than you? Where is the evidence that your hair is a mess? What if people love your 'bed-head' look?

If you have overslept and have missed the train to get to a meeting then yes, you are going to be late, but is you scolding yourself for doing so going to help you get to the meeting any sooner?

We rarely stop to reflect on our thoughts, and we rarely question ourselves when we make assumptions about the negative stuff. It just is, because that's the way it always has been, and we believe it, and if we continue to think the same things, we aren't making space for creativity or growth.

We all come to this planet with approximately the same number of brain cells, and as any self-respecting neuro-scientist will tell you, that little voice in your head is controlled by you, and nobody else. So change what it is saying to you.

Self-Awareness

The next time you speak negatively to yourself just stop! Then ask yourself where that negativity came from. Is there any evidence to back up what you're telling yourself? If we were all as incompetent and inefficient as we sometimes tell ourselves we are, we wouldn't be doing what we're doing.

Self-awareness is the basis for a better understanding of your individuality, and when you can clearly recognize your values and why they are important to you, you will have started to get some insights about how to align your personality with your work.

Clarify your values

Your values are who *you* are. They're not who you would like to be one day, they are the very essence of who you are right now.

Your values are your compass to finding a place in the world and in all areas of your life, where you feel fulfilled and comfortable.

Whenever you have an important decision to make, such as taking the next step in your business, maybe moving to a new city or even country, your values play a key role in how easy and successful that process is going to be for you.

If you try to tell yourself that you want something without understanding the 'why' behind it, or if you try to convince yourself that everything is going to work out just fine, even though there's uncertainty in your mind yet you can't quite put your finger on its source, you are not aligned with your values. And that means that you are not aligned with who you are.

For this exercise, it's important that you use a pencil. Writing in pen suggests to your brain that something is final, whilst writing in pencil will allow you to continue to make changes more easily – and I promise you that you are going to want to make changes as you go deeper into what really matters to you.

Keep this information close to hand so that you can add and change as you go through the book.

There is no right or wrong with values, and once you have decided which ones matter the most, you will have discovered your own boundaries, making it much easier for you to decide what your personal brand and image is going to be.

AND, this exercise is also going to give you some clarification about how to best market yourself when it matters, and to whom.

To help you get started with the following activities, here is a selection of values you might consider – the list is by no means exhaustive. You may find that some of them can be combined – for example kindness and compassion - just so long as you are clear on YOUR definition of the value in question.

Harmony	Trust	Kindness	Honesty
Friendship	Freedom	Team player	Accurate
Correct	Authenticity	Integrity	Honour
Reliability	Excellence	Creative	Achievement
Community	Faith	Autonomy	Contribution
Happiness	Authority	Leadership	Optimism
Recognition	Loyalty	Stability	Responsibility
Compassion	Religion	Spirituality	Fairness
Respect	Self-respect	Reputation	Balance

Activity: Values Worksheet
Create a list of your values in the middle column and add your definition (example given below). Then give your values a score between 1 and 10 using the column on the right (10 is high). When you have completed your list, rank each value (using the column on the left) in order of the importance you have placed against each item (from your column on the right).

Rank in priority order	Value/description	How important is this value to you? Score on a scale of 1 to 10 (10 is high)
	Loyalty – supporting me without question or judgement. Being on 'my side' in case of conflict or disagreement with others	

What are the obstacles?

We frequently compromise our values, depending on how strongly we feel about them. Increasing your awareness of the obstacles and challenges that result in you making those compromises will help you avoid them in the future.

Activity: Obstacles to Values

Complete the table below using the values you identified on the previous worksheet (one example has been included).

Value	How do you honour it?	What are the obstacles?	Obstacle score on a scale of 1 to 10 (10 is high)?
Loyalty	By being loyal to my family and friends	I sometimes put my job first because I want to do things properly at work.	7

Depending on how you have prioritised your values will impact on the action that you want to take. You will make some changes easily, and others are likely to take time. Be kind to yourself and understand too that you cannot change others (only you).

You must take full ownership of your values, so that you no longer have to compromise when you don't want to. You will never enjoy working with people who do not have similar values to you, and choosing your own boundaries is an important part in the personal branding process.

Activity: Actions for Change
Commit to the actions you're going to take to begin your re-alignment with who you really are and give yourself a deadline.

Value	Action to take	By when
Loyalty	Tell my family in advance if I have to work late Don't cancel on friends at the last minute Manage my work plan better	From now! From now! By December

Summary

You are capable of so much more than you think, and whilst it's a cliché to blame everything on your parents, many of your values and beliefs were formed before you were a teenager. By looking closely at your 'why' – and questioning whether your values and beliefs are yours – you'll find that you have been making a lot of assumptions about what is possible.

In Part Two of the Stepping Into You Blueprint I'm going to give you several tools that allow you to release the old and make some space for the new.

Part Two

RELEASE

Chapter 2 ~ The Scariest Relationship You Will Ever Have

"At the centre of your being you have the answer; you know who you are, and you know what you want." -
Lao Tzu

Who are you?

It is the most crucial question you must answer, and by the end of this part of the Stepping Into You Blueprint you will have had some meaningful conversations with yourself about what has prevented you from standing out from the crowd before now.

So – who are you? Do you even know? Do you know what you enjoy doing? Do you give yourself permission to enjoy what you do? When was the last time that you spent a day or even an hour doing something purely for pleasure, just for you?

You may be telling the outside world that you're quite happy with how things are, and that you don't *need* time to yourself. But is that true? And had you considered that every time you say *yes* to someone else, you could potentially be saying *no* to you?

As human beings we are brilliant at putting on a mask for others, telling them that everything is fine, when deep down we wonder what happened to the plans and dreams we had ten or twenty years ago. Some call it a mid-life crisis, although it depends upon your definition of mid-life.

Some recognize it as that moment when they tell themselves, 'There must be more to life than this'. Women in particular try to ignore this inner voice, telling themselves that they should stop being so stupid.

But ignoring those thoughts and controlling your emotions will only provide a short-term fix. The increasing prevalence of burnout, depression and worse, is evidence that we are not prepared to be honest with ourselves about what it is that we really want, and not allowing ourselves to be who we are.

When things don't feel quite right you may be inclined to blame your family or your friends or even the government. You could be telling yourself that you aren't clever enough or confident enough to do what you want (remember the 'imposter syndrome' from Chapter 1?).

Yet all those things are merely an attempt to push the focus outwards so that you can escape responsibility. In the long term, this approach is futile. If you have reached the point of being desperate for change, then it's likely that you have been ignoring your inner voice for a very long time.

So right now you have a choice. You can learn to care about and love yourself more than anyone or anything else, and acknowledge the fabulous being that you are, putting yourself at the top of your agenda.

Or you can decide that whilst change would be fabulous, you have been alright up until now with the *status quo*, and you're content to continue with things as they are.

Being authentic and aligning with your deepest desires are key to defining your personal brand. There is no wrong or right. Deep inside, you know exactly who you are, and the only relationship that has a significant impact on your life is the one you have with yourself.

Queen of Fabulous or Queen of Fear

When you hear the word 'courage', what image does that conjure up? There's a lot of talk these days on the subjects of personal growth and development, about being brave and all the rest of it, and that's fine – but I'd like you to look at it from a different angle.

If you talk about having to be courageous, you're coming from a place of weakness. Developing your personal brand requires you to start from a place of strength and to recognize the authority that you have in your life.

I appreciate that I might have to use my powers of persuasion to convince you that I'm right, so ask yourself these questions:
- Who is in control of you?
- Who decides what you think?
- Who decides what you can and cannot do?

Hopefully you will have got the same answer to all three questions. So you see, we're not talking about how brave you are. The conversation we need to have is about how honest you are with yourself, and what you are afraid of.

Fear of change

I have not met many people during my work who relished the thought of change. Some of them professed to being flexible and willing to adapt to new situations, but they were talking about small changes to their schedules, such as having to do a bit of overtime at work or helping a colleague if the workload was heavy.

As human beings, we love our comforts and routines and, whenever faced with change, we all go through a similar emotional process, but at different speeds. Fear of change becomes an issue when we get stuck in that process and to prevent that from happening, we need to check in with our emotions and learn how to manage ourselves effectively.

The late German-American Psychologist Kurt Lewin is heralded as being the founder of modern social psychology, and his theories and concepts continue to impact our lives today. Some of his most important work was around the subject of change, and how human beings behave when confronted with said change (https://www.mindtools.com).

Although Kurt Lewin's change management model from the 1940s is better known in an organizational setting, the three basic steps for personal change are the same.

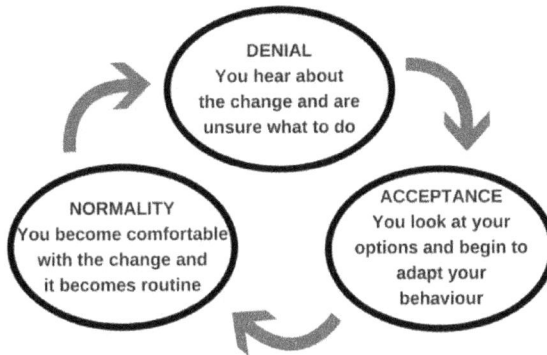

Adapated from Kurt Lewin's Change Management Model (Unfreeze - Change - Refreeze)

First, you hear about the forthcoming change, and your initial reaction is denial. You ask why it's necessary and you feel uncomfortable. Some people spend just a few seconds or minutes in this phase, because the answer to their 'why' question may have provided the necessary justification.

It's not always so simple though. In one instance a few years ago I was delivering a workshop on interview preparation. The participants had all known for months that they were going to be made redundant, and most of them were willing to put in the effort required to market themselves.

But one participant sat through the workshop and did nothing. After speaking with him it was clear that he was in denial and had convinced himself that senior management would keep him on because he was a nice chap and had worked hard. That type of a reaction can cause personal devastation.

Step number two in the process is that you begin to look for ways of dealing with the change, and you may even find that you adapt your behaviour to the forthcoming new situation.

For example, if a relationship goes wrong, after the initial heartbreak or split, the first thing that a lot of women do is to get their hair cut and buy some new clothes because they want to reinvent themselves. (It's only a temporary solution by the way, because change has to happen on the inside as well.)

The final step is that you become comfortable with the change, your new behaviour becomes habit, and everything feels normal – until the next change comes along and you start all over again.

So next time you find yourself faced with change, notice what your body is telling you. How much time do you take to go through each of the steps?

OK, so you may be telling yourself that it isn't change that you're afraid of, and you could be right. So let's take a look at the other types of fear that can cause sleepless nights.

Fear of failure

This type of fear is what the majority of people tell themselves is holding them back from being magnificent. They're afraid of disappointing others, or they're afraid of appearing and feeling foolish. They're afraid that they aren't clever enough or that they don't have the right skills or the ability to learn something new.

Other reasons I have heard from clients include that they are too old or too young, they're not good looking, they're no good at talking to others … the list goes on.

And even though all these things can seem like very real and insurmountable problems to those concerned, they can be broken down and resolved.

We'll get into the details of something fabulous called 'neuro-plasticity' later on, but for now just remember that all the negative chit-chat happening in your brain is only there because you've been listening to and telling yourself the same stories for years and years.

Because where's the evidence that you're going to fail?

Fear of success

Huh? Surely everyone wants to succeed, right?

Wrong. This is more common than you may think. I know because it's something I've experienced first-hand, and I hear it from others too.

One of my coaching clients had been working as a secretary for several years, and could do her job with her eyes closed. But she was at the point where she wanted to set up in business on her own so that she could work less and travel more.

Her idea of being a Virtual Assistant seemed like a logical option. She was very capable and efficient, and having managed an office for a long time she had a good idea about the services she could provide and to whom. But something was stopping her from making the move towards self-employment.

As we began working together she discovered that she was afraid of being judged as being better than others and not fitting in any more. Having come from a modest background she was also concerned about what her husband and family would say if she was earning a good salary because they had always been critical of wealth.

One of the issues in this type of situation is that friends and family who don't want to see you fail think that the best way to support you is to tell you that you should stay where you are. They're simply projecting their own fears onto you.

Another scenario is that they may be jealous of you branching out to do something that you love, something they wished they had done themselves.

It's no wonder that there is still a shortage of women in the boardroom or successful female business owners. We want everything to be harmonious and to keep everyone else happy, and we end up hurting ourselves.

Fear of money

Money – both having it and the lack of it – is probably the greatest cause of sleepless nights, yet the beliefs we have around money, most of which come from our parents and grandparents, tell us that money is bad and difficult to come by. You will have heard statements such as 'money doesn't grow on trees', 'save hard for a rainy day', or 'money can't buy you happiness'.

Your money stories can have a serious impact on your ability to do business. You may have the best entrepreneurial idea of the century, but if you can't ask others for money because you're not sure that they can afford what you're offering, or you feel uncomfortable marketing your services, you'll stay poor.

Our dislike of money is highlighted by the research around lottery winners. According to the statistics from Reader's Digest, "whether we win $500 million or $1 million, about 70 percent of us lose or spend all our money in five years or less."

Whilst we consciously say that we want and deserve more money, on a subconscious level we're telling ourselves that nice people don't have lots of it. Crazy but true.

Here's a quick test for you to find out how you feel about money. Ask yourself these questions and pay close attention to how you *feel* when you find the answers.

- How much money do you deserve to have?
- Who gets to decide what you earn?
- If you could charge whatever you wanted to, would you be charging more than you are now?

Activity: What are you afraid of?
Write down the stories you've been telling yourself about what could happen if you were to fail, or succeed and be fabulously rich, and then read what you've written out loud.

How real do your fears still seem?

It's time to get selfish

Before you move on to making the changes that will enable you to market yourself magnificently, there are two more things I want to touch on.

Please begin to be more selfish with how you spend your money and time, because even if you go to the gym or meditate in the morning, I'm betting there's not much that you do that is geared towards *your* professional success.

You deserve to spend time and money on yourself, regardless of your marital status, or whether you have a young (or old) family. Aim to devote at least 30 minutes each day to work on your personal brand, and save three per cent of your monthly income.

If you already looked at the download page you will have seen that there's a link to my 30-day action-plan which will help you begin implementing everything you have learned when you have finished this book. The activities vary in length, but consistent action is going to get you results fast!

Get yourself a piggy bank or a savings book or something where you can deposit the three per cent of your monthly income, so that by the time you have transformed into a magnificent marketer of you, you can celebrate in style.

So let's do a quick check in about where you are now so that you can measure your progress during the coming weeks and months. Much of how you feel about yourself is reflected in your home environment, even down to the state of your make-up bag and the fact that your shoes need re-heeling, again!

Take a close look at how you feel about your life and identify the things that are bringing your energy down. Use the activity on the next page to declutter whatever isn't working for you.

Activity: People and objects that drive you bonkers

Jot down how good or bad you feel about each of the following using a scale of 1 to 10 (10 is the best you can feel). Download the list here if it's easier for you :

http://bit.ly/SIY_The_Downloads

Outside of you

- Your work place
- Your colleagues
- Your car

You

- Your diet
- Your health
- Your quality of sleep
- The amount of time you spend on you
- The amount of money you spend on you
- Your work
- Your finances

Your home

- The entrance hall
- The colours and decorations in each of the rooms
- Your kitchen
- Your bedroom including the bedding
- The furniture in your home (go through every room paying special attention to your bathroom and bedroom)
- Your clothes
- Your underwear (when did you last treat yourself?)
- Your work clothes
- Your casual clothes

Recognize that wanting nice things isn't being materialistic. Although we're focusing on the internal work that needs to be done to nail your personal brand in this part of the Stepping Into You Blueprint, be aware that every time you put on those knickers that have been through the washing machine two hundred times, or the winter coat that you've had for ten years, if you don't love wearing those items, you are bringing your energy down.

Help yourself feel special about being you, and what you wear will make a big difference. So before you go on to the next chapter, which item of clothing makes you frown every time you look at it in your wardrobe?

Just bin it! (or take it to your local charity shop if you can't bear to throw it away).

Summary

Be honest about the relationship you have with yourself and acknowledge and accept how you may have been holding yourself back from success.

It's ok to feel fear if you are running away from a tiger, but being afraid of your failure or success is an emotion that needs to be released. At the very least, feel better about yourself by getting rid of an item of clothing that makes you cringe.

Chapter 3 ~ EQ And Ego

*"You have to change who you are on the inside,
for anything to change on the outside." -
Sandy Forster*

Have you heard the term 'emotional intelligence'? When you
have finished reading this chapter you will understand its
importance in helping you to feel comfortable when marketing
and promoting yourself.

Emotional intelligence – the theory

One of the first psychologists to describe 'non-academic'
intelligence was Edward Lee Thorndike, who identified the
concept of 'social intelligence' almost 100 years ago in 1920
(https://histoiredintuition.com).

Fast forward to 1990, when two researchers, Peter Salavoy of Yale
University and John D. Mayer of the University of New Hampshire,
developed the idea of 'emotional intelligence' (EI), and who
defined it as "the subset of social intelligence that involves the

ability to monitor one's own and others' feelings and emotions, to discriminate among them and to use this information to guide one's thinking and actions" (1990).

It was up to the better-known Daniel Goleman however, to shape EI to the popular model that we know today, and whose book with the simple title 'Emotional Intelligence' (1995) has sold over five million copies worldwide.

EI is being smart about your feelings. It's about managing yourself and managing how you behave in your relationships with others. It's also about understanding the judgements you make – about yourself and others - when you talk about someone 'showing off', or being egotistical, or being big-headed.

Every judgement we make comes from years of giving meaning to a situation or action, and we rarely stop to ask whether that judgement is fair or not.

Remember the question I asked you about who is in control of you? *You choose every emotion you experience*. You choose to get upset when you have an argument, you choose to be happy when you hear good news, and you choose to be angry when someone betrays you.

No one can make you feel anything unless you choose to do so. By the same token, you cannot persuade (or dissuade) anyone, or influence them to take action, unless *they choose* to do so.

Wouldn't the world be a better place if we all understood that every expression of emotion was of our own choosing, and that spending time sulking alone or blaming others are purely efforts to relinquish any responsibility for ourselves?

OK – it's likely to take a while for that to sink in because you're so used to trying to *control* how you feel. But when you own your personal power and learn how to manage the brand that is *you,* your life will transform, and even though there will still be ups and downs, one day you'll look back and realise how fabulous your life has become.

What is ego?

This is what the Oxford English Dictionary has to say about ego: "A person's sense of self-esteem or self-importance." And "The part of the mind that mediates between the conscious and the unconscious and is responsible for reality testing and a sense of personal identity."

Regrettably that three-letter word is so misunderstood and has been abused for such a long time, that it has the reputation of being something awful.

But you need your identity, right? So the trick is to learn how to manage it effectively so that the only people calling you egotistical are those who genuinely don't have a clue about how brilliant you are.

Your ego is one of the things that makes you completely unique but if it's in overdrive you will be called arrogant, and if you don't have enough of it, you'll constantly be thinking that other people are better than you. The easiest way to manage your ego is to increase your awareness of what you're feeling.

The next time you get into a discussion and you feel the need to prove your point at any cost, stop and ask yourself why. Is you being right going to be life-changing? If not, let it go.

In the same way, the next time that you see someone who appears confident, glamorous, beautiful and all the things you think you are not and never will be, challenge yourself and ask where the evidence is for that daft assumption.

Your feelings and your body will tell you whether you're right or wrong a long time before your brain kicks in to analysis mode and starts giving you logical arguments for and against.

Be kind to your ego, because you need it.

Self-praise?

This is where we start to move into the realms of what is real and what isn't, because in the words of John Assaraf, "it's only our perception that causes us to believe something is good or bad" (Assaraf, J. 2007 "Having it all") – and for the most part, self-praise is considered to be bad.

Activity: Identify Your Skills
Write down 12 things that you do really well. If you're not sure then ask your best friend what they think you're good at. This is an important exercise to help you nail your personal brand because by acknowledging that you're good at certain things, you will begin to feel more confident about what you offer.

It's a mistake to try to mould yourself to the needs of your clients, you MUST begin with focusing on what *you're* good at, what *you* love to do, and then find the clients that match those things.

For example, I'm useless at creating formulas in Excel, and I have a friend who can do in 10 minutes what could take me ten hours. When I asked for help they couldn't understand how anyone could *not* know how to use Excel because for them it's easy. In the same vein, when we first meet, many of my clients are petrified of sitting in front of a camera, so I teach them an easy to follow process that they can practice and which helps them to build their confidence (we'll talk about video in Chapter 10).

When doing this exercise with one of my clients, the only thing she could initially come up with was that she was very efficient. But she didn't consider that to be a skill. So then we turned things around and I asked her what would happen at work if she wasn't efficient. Answer – she would have chaos on her hands.

You have got loads of brilliant skills and abilities that you aren't even aware of because you do them so easily and take them for granted, yet for others they might be inexplicably difficult.

When you have got your list of 12, say them out loud to yourself. "I am good at …" or "I am a brilliant …". You may cringe the first few times, but I bet you that by the time you read out those sentences 20 times or more, you'll begin to feel different about what you do well, and may even feel a teeny weeny little bit proud of yourself.

The labels that you and others give you

What is the first thought that enters your mind when you wake up in the morning? Have you got to get up and let the dog or cat out, or make breakfast for your family, or check your emails or Facebook?

For each of those activities you step in to a different persona. Your dog thinks you're the pack leader (I'm not sure about cats), if you've got children then you're their Mum, your clients think of you as a business owner and/or service provider, and your Facebook friends could put you into any of those previous categories.

If you could choose, which label would you give yourself? If we were to fast forward six months or a year, what title will be on your business card?

Tomorrow morning when you wake up, think of yourself as a woman with unique abilities who loves what they do, knowing that you're going to have a fabulous day when everything works perfectly.

I'm not for one moment suggesting that you should ignore everything going on around you, I would just love you to focus on YOU for one or two minutes after you open your eyes, instead of going full steam ahead with being those other things. If nothing else, it will help you to start your day on a positive note.

Perception and reality

Perception is the reality of the person perceiving. We all have different realities. We all experience our lives in a way that is unique to us. In addition to living the different personas that I talked about above, no two people will ever see things the same way because it's not our eyes that are seeing, rather it's the messages that our eyes (the retina) transmit to our brains.

Even if you do your best to understand others, sometimes it's easier to let go of judgement. If you're not sure, work with evidence and facts, and remain unbiased, because you will *always* be interpreting situations and people from *your* perspective.

Here's a quick example: Imagine you dislike meeting a particular client at their offices because you are convinced that their staff is unfriendly and doesn't value your contribution. Now what if your client's team thought you were the best thing on the planet, but they're scared to talk to you let alone smile because they think you always look angry?

Your reality is created (perceived) by what you believe, and you will only ever be too big or too small, or too clever or too stupid when you waste time comparing yourself to others.

The next time a negative thought creeps into your conscious, stop it by turning your attention to something that makes you smile (I'll give you some great tools in the next chapter). Begin to create a different reality for yourself, based upon the gorgeous being that you are.

Hoping is a rubbish strategy

One of the reasons I decided to write this book was because I have seen too many women be passed over for promotion, or even give up on their dreams of being a successful entrepreneur.

In their book 'Women Don't Ask', Linda Babcock and Sara Laschever talk about the shockingly low statistics for women holding senior management or leadership positions. They also review the results of many studies which show that women don't negotiate for reasons such as not wanting to be seen to be assertive or aggressive.

It's a complaint voiced by my clients too, many of whom believe that they should win more business based on their qualifications and experience, and not their capacity to self-promote.

Whilst I don't like to place emphasis on the women versus men in the workplace debate, there is no escaping the fact that as a female business person you are going to have to work hard to find a balance between being authentic and staying true to your values, and feeling comfortable when you have to 'stick up for yourself' in negotiations around money and other male-dominated sectors.

Also remember that as long as you are working *against* something and constantly comparing yourself with others, you are going to be exerting energy that could be spent focusing on the things that really matter, ie., your personal brand and your business.

Summary

Hoping that someone, somewhere is going to notice how brilliant you are (or want to work with you based purely upon your qualifications) is a rubbish strategy, and I have never seen anyone who depended upon that approach succeed.

At the other end of the spectrum are those who believe that you have to behave like a man to get ahead, frequently resulting in upset. Comparing yourself to others can cause despair, so don't do it. Focus on what is important to *you* and what *you're* good at.

Chapter 4 ~ Dissolve Your Fears

"Everything you want is on the other side of fear." -
Jack Canfield

So how are you supposed to get rid of all that negative chit chat happening in your brain during most of your waking hours? Self-forgiveness and self-compassion are a great way to begin the process of releasing negative thoughts and feelings.

Although there is no magic wand – you won't make the changes overnight – when you release beliefs that no longer serve you, you will become aligned with who you are, and you can create a business that resonates with your true desires.

I have used (and continue to use) each of the processes below with great success. Some of them may seem too easy or even too ridiculous to work, but if you try them out knowing that you have nothing to lose (as I did), you'll soon begin to notice a shift in how you feel about yourself.

Ho'oponopono is a process of forgiveness originating in Hawaii and which has gained in popularity following its introduction to the western world by Joe Vitale (of 'The Secret' fame) who calls it "housecleaning for the soul"

Activity : Ho'oponopono

Begin by writing down EVERYTHING on a piece of paper that causes you to feel angry or resentful towards yourself (or others), and then go through each of the items on your list as you say (either out loud or in your head):

- I'm sorry
- Forgive me
- Thank you
- I love you

Cross out what you have written after saying the above. Once you have crossed it out, it's gone. Look forward. I have had clients look at me as though I was crazy when I've introduced this form of release to them, but the very act of writing what is upsetting you onto paper, gets it out of your brain and allows you to acknowledge it and let it go.

Next on my list of things to try is **'tapping'** – or 'emotional freedom technique'.

Jane Jackson, a fabulous teacher in all things tapping, kindly agreed to explain what is in more detail: "Emotional Freedom Technique (EFT) or Tapping is an energy psychology which blends Western "talk" therapy with the Eastern wisdom of "meridian points" or acupressure.

It works on a similar basis to acupuncture, but instead of using needles we tap with our fingertips on key acupressure points.

The energy meridian system is a bit like an internal energy map connecting all the different parts of our body. Sometimes blockages can occur in our energy system, leading to negative emotions and restricting our ability to live a harmonious life.

The theory is that negative events that we are exposed to in life can cause a blockage (disruption) in the energy system and as a result negative (sometimes intense) emotions manifest and can get locked into the body.

The resulting symptoms can be either emotional or physical. EFT works to clear such disruptions and eliminate the resulting emotional response or intensity to restore emotional harmony and offer relief from physical discomfort.

Tapping on acupressure points whilst talking about our issue helps us to connect to the blockage and release the flow of energy."

You can find Jane's contact details at the back of the book under 'resources' if you would like to know more.

Breathing is something that we all take for granted, but it is very effective pattern interrupter (it breaks the flow) when you feel the negativity beginning to rise. Your normal breathing pattern will probably be to inhale and exhale for the same amount of seconds, and if you meditate, you'll know that it's typical to count during the breaths you take, perhaps four in and four out.

To use breathing as a pattern interrupter, instead of counting even numbers as mentioned above, try breathing in for the count of three thinking good things, and breathe the bad stuff out for the count of five. If you do that even for one or two minutes you'll feel better.

Activity: Breathe

Close your eyes, and focus on your breathing. For two or three minutes, inhale for the count of three, and exhale for the count of five. How do you feel?

Meditation is no longer reserved for New Age/Alternative Therapies and science shows us that there is no right or wrong to meditation. Gone are the days of crossing legs and doing the 'OM' thing, and as little as 10 or 15 minutes of focused breathing can produce fabulous benefits to your mental and physical health.

Sit somewhere quiet where you won't be disturbed, and set yourself a timer for 15 minutes. Inhale for the count of three and exhale for the count of five whilst focusing on feeling good, or visualise the life of your dreams. Easy.

Your body is the most reliable source of knowing whether that little voice in your head is going into overdrive, because you will feel bad. It simply isn't possible to feel happy or contented if you are going against the grain of who you are, or if you're limiting yourself in some way.

Listen to your gut, your body, your instincts or whatever you want to call it, and as soon as you notice the negative chat getting louder, make a conscious effort to think about something good.

You'll soon begin to notice the changes, and it is nothing short of liberating when you realise how much power and choice you have over your future, instead of staying in victim mode.

How to create new beliefs

The breakthroughs in neuro-science during recent years have taught us that we are capable of learning new things during our entire lifetime, and the one pre-requisite to any type of change is to actually WANT to. Thereafter you must clarify your WHAT and your WHY.

The 'what' is this book, which just leaves the 'why'.

Why do you want to be able to market yourself with confidence?
Why do you want to be able to negotiate for your business?
Why do you want to be a multi-millionaire?

Understanding your 'why' will give you a sense of purpose, and every time you find yourself straying from your strategy or plan, it will remind you of why you started in the first place.

The way that our brains create new beliefs is like this.

Imagine you live in the mountains in a small village and one night it snows so much that you are cut off from the next town where you usually buy your groceries. Somehow you have to get to the town because you and your fellow villagers need food urgently.

Because you are the only person in the village who has a good set of snow shoes, you wrap yourself up in your big coat, thick scarf, hat and gloves, and set off with a rucksack on your back.

Your journey on foot is extremely difficult because the snow is so deep, it's freezing cold, and although you know the approximate direction of the town, you aren't sure that you are taking the right path because the wind is blowing snow into your face.

After a couple of hours of strenuous effort, you reach the town and are able to buy some provisions, but you can't carry too much because you only have the rucksack on your back, and you don't want to be carrying a lot of weight through the snow.

Thankfully however the return to your village is slightly easier than the outbound trip because you can at least retrace your steps made visible by the large snowshoes.

You have to do the same thing the next day, and the next, and the next, and after a week or so the footprints made by your snowshoes have created a narrow pathway.

By now though you are getting very tired of having to make the difficult journey every day and you starting to feel grumpy. Why is it down to you to do all the hard work? Why can't someone else do it?

Our motivation shrinks when we don't make progress fast. Whenever you start something new – a fitness regime, or writing a book, or developing your personal brand – the initial enthusiasm will wane at around day 10 or 11. It just all seems too difficult.

But then you remember your 'why', you remember how much you love living in the village, and you continue to walk to and from the town each day.

The weather is still bitterly cold, but eventually it stops snowing, and some of the other villagers come with you so that you are able to buy more provisions and carry some fuel for burning.

Every journey makes the pathway wider and easier to walk on. A couple more weeks pass, and despite a few snow flurries, your pathway is beginning to look like a narrow road, and quite soon you and the other villagers can drive, albeit slowly, to buy food and other items that you all need.

The weather improves and everyone is still using the new road to travel to town, and when the snow begins to melt and the old road is revealed, you all see that the previous route was much longer and not as pretty.

After some discussion you and your neighbours agree to allow the old road to remain un-used, and eventually everyone forgets about it.

In real-life it would work like this. Imagine you have been going to the gym for five or six weeks and you are beginning to see great results, and then one of your friends from overseas comes to visit and wants you to spend all your time with them eating pizza and ice-cream, watching box-sets on the television and reminiscing about the good old days – because that's what you always do when they visit.

You might be tempted to do just that, because you love spending time with your friend. But then you remember why you have been following your fitness regime, and how great you're feeling about yourself, and you say 'no' to pizza and ice-cream – and your friend says that they feel insulted and upset, and it's all your fault.

And it's precisely because we don't want to upset others that we stop giving priority to our well-being – we just carry on doing as we've always done because it's easier than having to walk a new road, even if we're miserable doing it.

In the same way that you can make a path through the snow, you can create different habits and beliefs by building new neural pathways in your brain, by repeating actions or words or thoughts. One day at a time.

There will be days when you remember the old way of doing things, and wonder whether it might be easier to go back to more familiar territory, but you'll also have the option of sticking with your new habits; doing things differently and doing them better.

So which activities are going to help you re-wire your brain? As is the case with traditional and alternative medicine, you are going to have to decide what works best for you, and you will know what it is because you will feel good doing it.

EFT (or tapping) that I talked about above can also be used to create new beliefs, and if it's something you would like to know more about I would strongly suggest that you either get in touch with Jane Jackson (contact details at the back of the book), or find someone local to you (please make sure that you get recommendations first).

Right up there on the scale of things that I love most, along with tapping, is the practice of writing affirmations, because they are very easy and quick to do once you have the right words in place.

The first rule of affirmations is that they must always be positive. The second rule is that they must be personal to you (you can't go around wishing things for other people), and the third rule is that they must be in the present tense.

So for example if you find yourself holding your head in your hands saying, "I'm never going to be successful", you would turn that around into "I am a fabulously successful business woman".

And then you develop it further to "I am a fabulously successful business woman and am the 'go to' expert for personal branding".

There is loads of information on the internet about how to best do this, and John Assaraf (http://johnassaraf.com) recommends that you fill up an A4 piece of paper with your affirmations, at least once each day, and more if you want to.

You can also read your affirmations out loud to yourself. The main thing is that you repeat, repeat and repeat some more, because as you already learned at the beginning of this chapter, beliefs are purely thoughts that you have thought several thousand times.

Other things you could try are to write a journal as if you and your business were already where you wanted to be, or to create a vision board with pictures of your ideal office, ideal client, and ideal bank balance.

Set business and personal goals that are SMART

OK up until now, everything in this chapter has been about what's going on inside your head, and we need to take a moment to look at the traditional way of setting goals in the context of what you want for you, for your personal brand, and for your business, by being 'SMART'.

Specific

Always, always "begin with the end in mind" (Stephen Covey, 2004). If you know where you're going, you have a better chance of getting there and exactly in the way that you programme your SatNav to get to you to an address, you must know your end goal. Be very, very specific and answer these questions:

WHAT do I want?

WHY do I want it?

HOW is it going to help me fulfil my dreams?

WHO is involved?

HOW will I feel if I don't achieve it?

Measurable

Be honest. Where are you now with your personal brand, with your business, with your life? On a scale of 1 to 10, (10 is high), how confident are you that you are already marketing yourself magnificently? How confident are you that you are working with the right people? How are you going to know that things are getting better for you? Set out your current situation in writing so that you are able to clearly see the progress you make as you go through the Stepping Into You Blueprint.

Achievable/Attainable

You don't need to have all the details right now on HOW you're going to achieve your goals, but you do need to have a fair idea about the financial and human resources you require and which constraints you potentially face. For example, don't set yourself up with goals that require a significant contribution from others. Have goals that are within your control.

Realistic/Relevant

Are your goals relevant? It might seem a ridiculous question to ask, but how do your goals fit in with the bigger picture?

Time bound

Give yourself realistic deadlines for specific activities and put time in your diary for the actions you need to take to get you to your goal. Also ask yourself what could prevent you from getting everything done as you plan. For example, given the choice between going for dinner with friends and working on your social media, which one would you choose?

If you haven't already done so, now is definitely the time to download my time management tool here:

http://bit.ly/SIY_The_Downloads

Do whatever it takes to build new neural pathways with fabulous new beliefs, be that using meditation, writing affirmations, dancing around the bathroom to high vibe music, smiling at the ceiling, reading success stories about other people, setting yourself amazing goals - just do what makes you FEEL GOOD.

And finally, if you're someone who currently feels horrible asking for money from your clients, remember that when you market yourself and your business, you are not tricking anyone, and you aren't forcing anyone to part with their money unlawfully.

You are offering them the gift of what you do brilliantly, so that they get the results that they want. It will always be their choice to say yes. Get tapping and give yourself permission to succeed!

Summary

You have done some important work here towards stripping away the beliefs and habits that are cluttering your life and preventing you from reaching your full potential. The scariest relationship you will ever have is the one you have with yourself, but I promise you that it can also be the greatest love affair of all time.

Onwards!

Part Three

TRUST

Chapter 5 ~ Frequent Feedback is Fabulous

"Even negative feedback can be a gift. Take it seriously but don't let it define you. Define yourself." –
Jeff Weiner, CEO at LinkedIn

Feedback is one of those things that is always there, regardless of whether it's being articulated in words, or suggested by facial expressions and body language. There's simply no getting away from it, and this chapter is going to show you why it is one of the most valuable contributors to your success that you could wish for.

Criticism is your new best friend

A strong personal brand will ensure that you work with people who are on the same wavelength as you, but there will be times when you receive feedback from those who don't like your approach.

It's up to you to decide *whether* you want to use the feedback you receive, and if so, *how* you are going to benefit from it.

At the beginning of 2017 I worked with a designer to change my company logo, from a purple dove, to the more fluid figure you will have seen containing pink, red and gold.

I knew that not everyone was going to like my new corporate colours, and the reactions were varied. Several people said there was too much pink on my website, but pink is my favourite colour, and a lot of my clothes are pink, and if someone doesn't like that colour, then they probably aren't going to want to work with me.

It was a deliberate move, one of the goals of which was to de-clutter the individuals who would sign up for every freebie but who were not my ideal clients and it worked.

As you move through the Stepping Into You Blueprint, remember that there are some people out there who will openly criticise you, because a lot of the work around building your personal brand and marketing yourself magnificently will involve using social media. You may not be pleased with some of the responses you receive and thankfully it has become very easy to delete comments and block abusers.

We'll go into a lot of detail about promoting yourself online as we go into part four of the Stepping Into You Blueprint – THRIVE - but I want you to ingrain this next sentence in your brain, or stick it on a post-it note on your laptop. Remember that YOU are in control of what YOU do, and no-one can make YOU feel anything you don't want to.

Subjectivity is gold

If you ask ten people to give you an opinion on something, you'll get ten different answers. But when you nail your personal brand, you begin to narrow down the differences.

Right now there is one sure-fire method of gathering a varied response as to what people think about you, and that is to set up a survey for your family and friends, allowing them to answer your questions anonymously. Do it this week, and then again in a few months' time, and see what has changed.

Activity: Get Feedback From Your Friends and Family

One of the easiest ways to create a survey is to use the online tool (the basic version is free), SurveyMonkey, because you can send a link in an email.

Send the email to as many people as you want to, explaining that you're working on strengthening your personal brand because you want to be able to market yourself and your business effectively, and to the right people.

Tell them too that you appreciate their honest and constructive feedback, and if you're unsure about the reactions you may get, you could add that this is not an opportunity for them to sling mud at you. Give them a deadline so that you're not waiting for weeks on end for people to respond.

These are the questions you're going to give them:
- What do you think I'm good at?
- What do you think I'm not so good at?
- Which three words describe my positive/negative traits/ characteristics?

And then wait!

Giving yourself feedback

If you're anything like me, you will always be your own worst critic, which is great, as long as you use that criticism to keep learning and getting better at what you do. Ask yourself these three questions at the end of each week:

- What went well?
- What didn't go so well?
- What could I do differently/better next time?

You'll notice that I have used the word 'could' in the third question and not 'should'. It's another little bit of psychology that will help you to find solutions more easily. When you say 'what *should* I do', your brain begins to look for a single answer, whereas if you say 'what *could* I do', your thought process will help you to come up with several options.

Summary

As you develop your personal brand and your business, remember that feedback and criticism are going to provide you with invaluable insights about how to better serve yourself and those you work with.

Feedback can motivate, it can help you to improve your performance, and as you become more skilled in learning from your achievements and your mistakes, it will help you grow. It's your choice as to who you listen to, and it's up to you to decide how you'll use the feedback you receive.

Chapter 6 ~ The Future You

"Proper Planning and Preparation Prevents Poor Performance" - *Stephen Keague*

Like any transformational change, it all begins with getting clear on what you're creating. It's time for you to begin building a detailed picture of the Future You.

Activity: The Future You
Imagine that it's 12 months from now, and in as much detail as possible, visualise what you look like, what you're wearing, what you're doing, which type of people you are working with and where, which type of car you're driving, and anything else that comes to mind. Write down everything that you see and feel.

Finding out what you do well

In part two of the Stepping Into You Blueprint I asked you to write down 12 things that you enjoy and do really well.

Activity: What You Do Well

Go back to your notes and then answer these questions:

1. Why is that skill important to the work you do (to answer simply turn it around, if you didn't have that skill, what would be the result)?

2. What is it specifically that *you* enjoy about that skill? Is it the results that you get, or the process involved, or something else?

3. How do you approach using that skill? For example if you were planning an event, would you pick a date, book a room and start marketing, or, before doing any of that, would you begin by thinking about the type of people you wanted to attend, how many you wanted to participate, and what type of environment would best suit the topic?

Do you see the difference? You will have a unique approach to everything you do, and your distinctive style + your offer will be what makes others want to work with you.

Before that little voice in your head starts a conversation, think about why you go food shopping in a particular shop. You probably have the choice of around 10 major retailers within 15 miles of where you live, as well as your local offer in the form of a baker or a butcher or small grocery store, yet you choose to go to just two or three. Instinctively you will shop where you *feel* most comfortable.

Whilst your offer is important, it is how you make others FEEL that will make them want to work with you.

Once you are clear on those 12 skills, download your 'Personal Branding Content Library' template from this link: **http://bit.ly/SIY_The_Downloads**

Insert your skills into the template, putting them in the order of things that you enjoy doing the most, and then find some real-life, specific examples that clearly demonstrate how you do what you do.

Here's an example of what you might write if you loved to write copy for marketing and advertising.

Skill: Copy writing
Example: Worked (wrote the copy) with the company Beautiful Hair on their campaign to promote their new line of shampoos which resulted in them netting sales of £5,000 during the first three days after launch.

For each of your 12 skills, think of one or two examples such as that above, and keep adding to the Personal Branding Content Library from now on. Every time you get positive results with a client, make a note of which skills you used and how they contributed to the outcome.

Starting this process may feel as though you're putting your brain into overdrive, but it's purely the beginning of a new habit because you haven't been used to focusing on what you do well. Before you know it, you'll wonder how you could have ever doubted that you were doing great stuff every day.

You'll take the third step in this exercise later on in the Stepping Into You Blueprint. For now, well done !

Appearance is everything – the woman in the mirror

We have talked a lot about the fabulous being inside you, and now it's time to start looking at the outside, because when it comes to promoting your personal brand professionally, image is everything.

Be aware that every time you step out to the supermarket, or pick up the newspapers on a Sunday morning, you could bump into a client (or potential client), so make sure that your hair and what you are wearing matches your professional persona, always.

Before you go anywhere, look at yourself in the mirror and ask yourself what a potential client would think of you and if you don't like the answer, do something about it.

Colours

The colours you wear have an impact not only on the way that you look, but also on how you feel, and I would highly recommend that you make the investment to find a consultant who will be able to advise you on any changes you need to make.

During my own re-branding exercise, when I chose a new logo for my business, I began by meeting with Victoria Lochhead, Personal Stylist and owner of Frankie and Ruby (you can find her contact details at the back of the book), to find out which colours would best suit me.

I wanted consistency between what I was wearing and my marketing materials, and it was a massive relief to find out that pink was a match, but a disappointment to find out that cream and beige just weren't me (my summer wardrobe vanished).

Victoria's input had a big impact on the colours I now use. As she says, "Like it or not, what you choose to wear sends out salient messages about who you are. Others will pick up these visual cues within about four to seven seconds of meeting you and they'll make an instant decision about whether they can trust you. If you're representing your business, it's so important to get this first impression right as it literally can affect whether you succeed or fail.

Wearing colour, shapes and styles that reflect your natural self and the brand values of your business mean that your visual image is in alignment; nothing conflicts and therefore you will instantly come across as more likeable, trustworthy and easier to understand.

Using colour is the single biggest, quickest and easiest way to affect your visual image and begin dressing deliberately to convey your personal and brand messages."

Clothing

Developing your personal brand requires some tough decisions. When you did the decluttering exercise in part two you hopefully got rid of at least one item of clothing that you didn't like.

Go back to your wardrobe and make an honest assessment of everything else. If you don't love it or you haven't worn it for a year, get rid of it. If you decide to invest in a colour consultation, find an expert who will also advise you on style *before* you buy any new items of clothing.

Alternatively, most reputable stores offer a personal shopper service with their own style experts. Make an appointment on a day when you have no other commitments so that you can place your entire focus on your image.

Shoes

How do you feel when you put your shoes on? Your shoes will make a huge difference to how you show up in public, and if you're only wearing them because they're still serviceable, donate them to charity or bin them. Your need to feel fabulous about everything you wear.

Hair

Do you like what's happening with your hair at the moment? Have you had the same hairstyle and/or colour for the past 10 or 15 years? Can you manage your hair easily? How you feel about your hair also has the potential to transform the way you present yourself to others and even a quick trim could put a spring into your step if needed.

Take a photograph of yourself today and put it in a box for safe-keeping. You are going to be amazed at your transformation when it's done.

Summary

Create a future vision of yourself being an expert in your sector. Determine how you feel about your external image, and if you don't like it, get help.

Chapter 7 ~ Who Do You Want To Impress?

"You were born to win, but to be a winner, you must plan to win, prepare to win, and expect to win" –
Zig Ziglar

In Chapter 9 I'll help you put together a profile – sometimes known as your elevator pitch - that you can use when you're meeting new people and which focuses on your unique selling points, but for now just concentrate on getting a feel for the type of people you want to work with.

Who is your ideal client?

This is one of the craziest things I learned when I went into business, because it felt completely counter-intuitive, but be very, very specific about who you want to work with. Most importantly your clients' values and beliefs are going to have to be similar to yours.

If you try to be all things to everyone who asks, you'll end up being a nobody in business.

For example, I love working with female entrepreneurs and business owners, but I also want them to be committed to themselves and their goals, I want to have fun working with them, and I want them to be motivated enough to take positive action so that they get results. If a client doesn't meet those conditions then I know I'm going to have a hard time helping them.

Activity: Your Five Star Client

What are the characteristics of the person you would love to work with? Who is your five-start client? How old are they and where do they live? What do they do in their free time and where do they love to go on holiday? You can download my template for deciding on your ideal client **http://bit.ly/SIY_The_Downloads**

Another way to decide on your ideal client is focus on the characteristics of your friends. Write down everything about them that you love, respect and admire. When you have completed the template, give your five-star client a name and keep that person in mind every time you are promoting yourself and your business (more about that when we get onto social media in Chapter 10).

Be a private investigator (part 1)

You may already have clients, or you may just be starting out. Regardless of what you think you know about the person you are going to present to or work with, always take the time to do some research.

Even if you decide to do nothing else to change how you market yourself, this step will create a great impact on how you connect with those that matter, because you have a clear picture of your five-star client.

Activity: Check Out Your Potential Clients:

What is your first impression of their website and how does their web page make you feel? A well-laid out website that is easy to navigate will tell you whether the person or company is customer-oriented or not. That could be an important factor in your working together.

Which type of language is being used and does it feel easy to read? In addition to finding out what is important to the business, you can also learn a lot by reading between the lines of the mission statement or the history of the company. Do you think that they have paid a professional copy writer, or does the text sound as though someone has quickly written a few lines for the sake of having something for visitors to read?

How many photographs are on the site, and are there pictures of the people working there? We have already talked about the importance of image, and if you find yourself looking at photos of people with weird haircuts who are dressed casually, that will give you an insight about the business culture. Does it match yours?

Is there an 'about me' or 'about us' page? How do they describe themselves? Can you imagine what it's going to be like working with them?

Which social media platforms are they on, and which type of people follow them?

I'm not suggesting that you stalk anyone online, but you can glean so much useful information from the internet, and I promise you that 80 per cent of other entrepreneurs simply don't bother, giving you a strong advantage.

It's always about them

So now that you have decided what type of client you want to work with, the next step is to match your skills and abilities – and specifically your unique selling point (USP) – to what that person or business wants.

Of course you want to enjoy what you're doing which is why you did all the work to establish what you're good at, but when it comes to marketing yourself, you must also consider the standpoint of your client.

Whenever you introduce yourself or make the pitch for their business, they are going to be asking themselves "why should they work with you", and you must know the answer.

So think about how what you are offering is going to make a difference. What is the result that you promise that is going to contribute to their success? Why *should* they work with you and no-one else?

In the same way that you have defined how you want to feel working with a client, how are *they* going to feel working with you?

You are going to repeat this next exercise for every new contact you make because it is going to have a huge impact on the quality of your client base and your business success.

Activity: Is There a Match?

Look at the type of business that your potential client works in, identify key words that describe what they do and the results they offer, and then check whether those key words can be matched to your skills and examples that you included in your personal branding content template.

If the answer is yes, great. But if the answer is no, don't bother spending another second of your energy on trying to win them over, because it's not going to happen.

Summary

You owe it to yourself to work with clients that you like. Don't waste time trying to mould yourself to the needs of others. If you feel the slightest doubt, move on.

Chapter 8 ~ Storytelling Makes The Sale

"If history were taught in the form of stories,
it would never be forgotten." -
Rudyard Kipling

When you were a child, did you enjoy being told stories? Did you have a favourite fairy tale that you loved to hear time and time again? And now that you're older, do you enjoy going to the cinema and losing yourself in another world for a couple of hours?

Your brain loves a good story

Stories help your brain to get into gear to learn and discover, and you are more likely to remember a good story than someone reciting a list of facts (lists send most people's brains to sleep).

Stories motivate and inspire you, and give you not only a glimpse of new possibilities, but also how fabulous life would be if your dreams came true.

Why is that?

Stories evoke feelings, and feelings create emotional connections, and emotional connections help us make decisions about which action to take.

Storytelling makes the sale because it creates an emotional connection with your audience – even when there's no happy ending.

Although we all look to facts and figures and other hard evidence to justify our decisions, in that second when the decision is made, it is based on emotion.

When you tell your potential client a story about how you have helped another business with your services, you are giving them a taste of how they too could *feel.*

In a day and age when we have access to a limitless number of films on our televisions and tablets, we still love to go to the cinema. When the lights are turned down and your focus is on the big screen, you are taken on a journey to places you have never been to before, transported to a world where you have no responsibility or worries.

All your senses are responding to the story as it unfolds, encouraging you to identify with the film's characters. And there will usually be one character who the film makers want to be your hero.

If you have enjoyed the film you leave the cinema feeling inspired or motivated, and you want to keep that feeling for as long as you can, so you begin to think about ways in which you could bring that story to life. You want to find a way to be like the hero of the film.

Every time a James Bond film is released, Omega issues a new limited-edition watch, because they know that there are going to be a lot of men who want to feel just like 007.

When we watch films about successful women such as Coco Chanel, or chick-flicks such as Sex and the City, we go out and buy expensive clothes and shoes so that we too can succeed and have fun with our friends, or meet the man of our dreams. We want to identify with our role models regardless of whether they exist only in fiction, or in reality.

When you consider these actions in the cold light of day it seems slightly bonkers, but I never tire of looking at my beautiful, hot-pink, peep-toe Jimmy Choo shoes because they make me feel fabulous. I'm just waiting for the appropriate occasion to wear them!

It's all about *feelings*, and for many – although not consciously – a good tale takes us back to our childhood when all was well in the world and we listened to a bed-time story.

Yes, your qualifications are important and yes, your work experience will have to be relevant to your marketing, but it is going to be the stories that you tell that will help you to stand out.

How can you use storytelling to market yourself?

Go back to your Personal Branding Content Library and re-examine the examples you wrote down next to your skills. Instead of wracking your brain about what your achievements were, this time think about all the challenges you have helped others work through.

Regardless of your title or sector, you are a problem-solver, and you are helping your clients to fix things, and when you do that successfully, you make them *feel* better.

When you get home at the end of the day you may share your stories about your experiences – how you had a great meeting, solved a few problems for the people you met, and won some new business - with your family and friends.

Get into the habit of making a note of what those stories are and which problems you solved, and then add them into your Personal Branding Content Library.

Be aware of *how* you describe what you've done during the day because by using the same language and tone you'll come across as beautifully authentic when you market yourself.

In Chapter 7 you identified the type of people you want to work with based upon how they make you feel, and you also thought about what it is that you offer to make them choose you over anyone else.

It is the *emotion* you create in your stories that will make you a fabulous storyteller, and by connecting to your business contacts on an emotional level, your storytelling will help you make your sale.

The storytelling formula

There is a simple formula that you can follow for every story you tell from now on which is going to help you nail the sale. I call it the 'Five C's'.

Before you start, be clear on who your hero is going to be. Who do you want your clients to identify with? It's probably not going to be you, rather your hero is going to be either another client who has already experienced great success as a result of your fabulous support, or it will be the client you are working with/pitching to.

1.   Context – set the scene of where your story is happening and introduce the hero.

For example:
I help female entrepreneurs (coaches, trainers, service professionals etc) to nail their personal brand so that they feel comfortable marketing themselves and so that they can successfully turn their passion into prosperity.

2.   Crisis – what is the BIG problem that requires your input?

For example:
The number one complaint I hear from my clients is that they hate to talk about themselves,

I recently worked with a client who has been struggling to increase her audience and she was seriously considering giving up her dream. She provides a fabulous service to other women helping them to improve their fitness levels so that they have more energy for their work – we know how that feels, right?

3.   Course of action – what is it that you do to make things better?

For example:

We started by looking at what was most important to her about her business and to make sure that her personal values are aligned with what she does, because if you're faking it you're going to have a hard time making it.

She discovered that she wanted to drop a couple of elements of her service because she didn't find them fun let alone exciting. We revised her branding and marketing strategy, with an increased focus on the bits about her business that she loved.

4.   Challenges – even the best laid-out plans experience wrinkles and by including a couple of challenges you will further strengthen the emotional connection.

For example:

Of course, when anyone makes changes to their business there will always be an element of risk involved, and my client lost a few customers, because they didn't like her revised offer. But it was a risk that we talked about upfront, and the payback for letting go of what wasn't working for her was significant because she has already begun to attract a different calibre of customer, people that she loves to work with.

5.   Celebration – you're the best, you help your client win every time!

For example:

A breakthrough requires a lot of honesty and willingness to change which is why I stick with my clients every step of the way. And seeing the personal transformation of my client, and watching her go beyond her goals in her business is fabulous! Clearly those are my words, and you will use language that best suits your situation, but with practice, if you stick with that structure, you'll tell a great story every time. And the best bit about storytelling?

Because you're describing how you helped someone else and supported their needs and resolved their challenges, you will find marketing yourself much simpler. You won't have to use the word 'I' so often, and you will automatically feel more comfortable when talking about your achievements.

Summary So Far

Fabulous !! You have now completed the internal work of the Stepping Into You Blueprint by taking a close look at who you are, how others perceive you, and what it is that has been holding you back from showing up in the world as the authentic you, with a business that is aligned with your values.

You now know:
- How to better manage your time
- How to overcome fear
- Which items (and people) you need to declutter from your life
- What your values are, why they are important to you, and how they will help you to align with your business
- How to create new beliefs that better serve your fabulous future
- How to take responsibility and ownership for your business goals and success
- Who you want to work with – your five-star client
- How to create an emotional connection using storytelling

Before you move onto parts four and five of the Stepping Into You Blueprint, remember that there is no right or wrong to what you want to do.

You are not the person that you were yesterday, or a week ago, or a year ago.

Life is fluid, and even though you have already made a lot of decisions about the direction that you want to go in, it's ok to change your mind and do something different, just so long as you're doing it because YOU want to.

Part Four

TRANSFORM

Chapter 9 ~ What's Your New Story?

"Being yourself is the only way to stand out in today's
crowded market. So what's YOUR story?" -
Magnetic Silvia

Whilst the work here can't be done overnight, you have already done most of the heavy lifting.

You have now reached the very practical elements of the Stepping Into You Blueprint which is set out in an easy to follow step-by-step process. Some things will work brilliantly for you first time around, and some won't, and you will want to refer back to your plans and activities to give them the polish that is going to make the brand that is you, unique.

There are no mistakes and there is no failure, only opportunities for you to learn so that you're better today than you were yesterday.

Take a deep breath, remember *why* you're doing this work, and then dive in.

Your Elevator Pitch

The first step of TRANSFORM is to create your 'elevator pitch', so called because it should be short (around 30 seconds) which is approximately the amount of time you might spend with someone in an elevator if you were going to the top floor of a building.

There are a couple of reasons for your elevator pitch having to be 30 seconds or less.

Firstly, if you can't grab someone's interest within 30 seconds (regardless of how long your conversation may be), they will stop listening actively to what you have to say and their mind will drift to other matters.

That sounds harsh, I know, but it works the other way as well. Think about how quickly you judge others based on what they're wearing or what they're doing, before they have even opened their mouth to talk to you.

Secondly, if you see someone at an airport or a train station (or somewhere else where they are likely to be in a hurry) that you met at an event but didn't get the opportunity to talk to and you want them to get in touch – but they're late for the flight or train – you need to get that message out quickly, loud and clear. No time for small talk about the weather!

You are going to need several variations of your elevator pitch because sometimes you'll be using it socially or informally, and sometimes you'll be using it full on to sell your services or products.

You know that you have already done a significant amount of work on this step by completing your Personal Branding Content Library, and in Chapter 8 I also gave you an easy-to-follow formula for telling your sales story.

In addition to you getting comfortable about introducing yourself, this next piece of work is going to form the basis for all your social media profiles.

Why do you want them to remember you?

When you are creating your elevator pitches, be clear on what it is that you want to achieve. What do you want the person with whom you are talking to remember about you? If it's for work it could be your unique skill set, but if it's for social reasons, it might be a hobby or sport that you enjoy.

Think of all the situations when you might need to impress someone quickly, and put them into three columns on the second sheet of your Personal Branding Content Library: *formal, informal, other.*

What do you do in terms of results?

Look back over your Personal Branding Content Library, Which skills would you like to highlight? If you do several things, for example you're a coach, a consultant, and a social media expert, which of those will you want to include?

Here's an example:

X   *I have a licence to work as a business consultant in Austria and I'm a qualified coach.*

√   I work with female entrepreneurs who want to nail their personal brand so that they can market themselves with confidence and achieve stunning results for their business.

Note that I could replace the word 'female entrepreneurs' with 'women', or 'female business owners' or 'senior managers'. You have already worked out your target audience. What type of people fall into that category?

- Never list, because lists are always going to be boring.
- Don't give them details such as information about your education/qualifications (you'll waste valuable time).
- DO include achievements or statistics that demonstrate your success, and the value that you could contribute.

Your Unique Selling Point (USP)

You must clarify which of your selling points (abilities and/or skills) are going to be the most relevant, according to the needs of the business or person you are pitching to, so although we talk about a *unique* selling point (or USP), it might be different from one client to the next.

This is why it is important to continue to update your Personal Branding Content Library including all those things that you're good at, and specifically which problems you are best at resolving (did you get past 12 yet?) in a variety of situations.

Your USP may be an aspect of your work experience (for example working in a multi-cultural environment, or working with fitness centres or restauranteurs), or it could be your approach to a particular skill.

When you have nailed the answer to this, you may believe that it's simply too easy to be relevant. But remember that it could be exactly *that one thing* that you do effortlessly that helps you get the job or business contract.

Start off by asking yourself *so what*, and *why is this important* for each of your skills, and then turn those questions around and ask yourself what would happen if you *weren't* good at what you do. You'll find that you very quickly begin to build a picture of how you contribute.

Here are a few examples of the questions you can ask yourself for some very basic skills that many of my clients didn't believe were relevant to their offer.

- **Efficiency** – what do you enjoy about being efficient? Does this mean that you're a process-oriented and/or results-oriented person? What would happen if you weren't efficient? What makes you good at it?
- **A problem-solver** – what do you enjoy about being a problem-solver? Does this mean that you're good at analysis and/or conflict resolution? If you weren't good at problem-solving what would the consequences be?
- **Creativity** – what is it about creativity that is important to you? Does this mean that you're the type of person who enjoys a lot of variety? What type of creativity do you like, and what results do you produce?
- **Communication** – this is a HUGE subject. How do you define communication? Writing? Speaking? Mediating? Listening? Managing? Creating lines of communication between team members? What is important about having good

communication skills? What would happen if you weren't good at communicating?

- **Planning/organising** – why is planning and organising important? What would happen if you weren't good at this? What do you enjoy about planning? Are you a person who focuses on details, or do you prefer to look at the big picture and let others get on with the little things?

With your USP, your elevator pitch develops further, for example:

I work with female entrepreneurs who want to nail their personal brand so that they can market themselves with confidence and achieve stunning results for their business. I have had great success with helping my clients to get comfortable with talking about themselves, and then showing them how to use storytelling to make the sale.

Remember that your Personal Branding Content Library is a living document, and you should be adding to it after every email exchange, telephone conversation and face to face meeting. *You* are your most valuable resource and keeping a record of your learning will contribute to increasing your confidence about what you can offer.

With practice you will be able to immediately decide which examples to use instead of umm-ing and ahh-ing, and then pinching yourself for not having said something important.

Finish with an open question related to the work you do

Don't be tempted to use the words 'so what do you do?' when talking to someone new. You could find yourself listening to a boring response citing a list of technical information. You want to encourage the person you're talking to, to tell a story, because that will help them to connect to you and your business further, so try one of these:

- *Business example*: so how does your business deal with its training/marketing/ accounting needs?
- *Work example*: so what is your approach to project management/recruitment/ conference (event) management?
- *Social example:* so how do you spend your (free) time?

Practise, practise, practise and then practise some more!

Don't break your brain by trying to memorise your pitch word for word.

Create the structure of your elevator pitches simply with bullet points. If you try to produce a narrative and then forget a word or two as you are speaking because you're nervous, you are going to put yourself under unnecessary pressure and could potentially lose the attention of the person you are talking to.

Record yourself with your laptop or mobile 'phone, and work out how much information you can include in a 30-second time span.

Talk to your reflection in the bathroom mirror. Get as close as you can to the mirror so that you can only see your eyes (not your mouth) and start talking. As you begin, your brain won't immediately compute that it's you talking, because you can't see your mouth. This is a great way to get used to listening to your voice.

Although this process might be slow to start with, when you begin to understand how much you have to offer and what you're really good at, AND you have already decided which USP to use for a specific situation, you will get better at introducing yourself to strangers very quickly, the result being that they will remember you for the right reasons.

And finally – if it's you breaking the ice and starting the conversation, the fastest way to connect with a stranger is to share or ask for some non-business related or personal information. I don't mean that you should be divulging your darkest family secrets, but don't go to the other end of the spectrum where you talk only business.

Beginning with a question such as 'have you been to that new restaurant down the street? I'm wondering about where to go for lunch' *or* 'I can't login to the WiFi – did you manage to connect?' *or* 'wow, I love your laptop bag/handbag/jacket – where did you buy it?', will work wonders in getting a conversation going, and you'll be able to easily keep talking after that because you have already prepared your elevator pitch.

Summary

Dig deeper into what it is you have to offer and determine why you want potential clients (and others) to remember you.

Chapter 10 ~ Your Online Brand

"To build a personal brand online you must be purposeful, not passive. If you build it, they won't come. If you build it and promote it, they will." – *Chris Smith*

In this chapter I'm going to give you a brief introduction to a number of social media platforms, and whilst each of them continue to evolve, their mainstream audiences are likely to stay the same, allowing you to choose which ones you want to use for your marketing.

I'll teach you how to put your marketing plan together (there's also a template for you), and remember that in addition to remaining focused on building a relationship with your potential clients, a critical component of marketing is consistency.

Social media still sends shivers down the spines of many business people (not just women) and if up until now you haven't been able to talk about yourself without feeling yucky, take this learning one step at a time.

Don't be tempted to spread yourself too thinly across the platforms. It's better to focus on one or two of them and do the marketing brilliantly, than attempt to post on 10 platforms and achieve very little.

In the unlikely event that you feel yourself going into overwhelm, please reach out to me either in my 'Stepping into You' Facebook Group because the work you do here is vital. If you're in business, an online presence is imperative, and websites, whilst important, don't cut it any more as a standalone means of marketing.

There are of course arguments for and against you being visible online, and I have worked with clients who found themselves the recipients of some unwanted attention, resulting in them being extremely apprehensive about their social media. Rightly so.

However, your personal brand already exists, and in an age where more than two billion people on the planet are on Facebook, we are at a stage where if you *don't* have an online presence, you run the risk of seriously weakening your business potential.

If your business partners can't find you online you will lose credibility. After all, who would want to work with another business that wasn't marketing itself and networking efficiently.

You can be almost sure that every time you meet someone at a business event or you ask them for a meeting, they will put your name into their search engine and see what comes up.

Personal security and safety first

In addition to talking about the types of audience, I want to start with some of the pitfalls of social media and how you can easily avoid them. First and foremost, you must understand that anything you put out on social media is like you advertising what you do on the front page of a newspaper.

Whilst governments all over the world are still working on their legal frameworks to effectively manage how data is collected and kept, as well as preventing online abuse, if you post something on the internet, it's out there for everyone to find. Even with the European General Data Protection Regulation (GDPR) in place, there are still unethical people who won't comply.

You already know that you shouldn't publish anything on social media about checking in at the airport for your holiday because some thieves will take it as an open invitation to burgle your home in your absence.

If people know that you live on your own, I would encourage you to apply those same principles when travelling for business. It's one thing to be talking about speaking at an upcoming event. It's quite another to announce to the world that you're flying to Las Vegas to attend a week-long conference.

You must take control of what others can find out about you to the extent possible, so that you not only protect yourself from unwelcome attention, but so that you also ensure that your online image matches your professionalism.

Your website and domain

Your website is the one place where you have complete control over how you showcase everything you do, including those hugely important testimonials from clients. Your domain should be relevant, as short as possible, and easy to remember.

If you already have a website then great! If you don't, also great, because these days it is very easy and very cheap to create your own, even if you have no clue about technology.

Your website is a *very personal part* of your business and needs to reflect *who you are*. As with all your other marketing, it isn't just about pictures and text, it's about how you want visitors to your site to *feel* and it will require regular updating with your vlog/blog and other content – and YOU need to be able to have full control over that process if you want to.

You may decide that you want some initial help when creating your site (if you don't already have one) to get clear on its purpose and how it should be laid out. Crucially, you'll be wanting to use the same colours and fonts as you do with all your other branding and a really useful exercise is to create a style guide that you (and in the future others) can refer to ensuring consistency in all your marketing (you'll find a template on your downloads page here: **http://bit.ly/SIY_The_Downloads**).

A basic site will be made up of four or five pages, for example 'home', 'about', 'what other people say', and 'contact' (be sure to check the legal requirements on the use of cookies and analytics/tracking which you can easily find on the internet).

There are several easy options from which you can choose to host your website, such as WIX or WordPress, or 1&1 or GoDaddy, and as with anything else I'd suggest that you look around before making a decision about which platform will best suit your needs. Just remember that before you sign up for anything, clarify how your website is going to contribute to your marketing. If you want to upload a lot of graphics and videos for example, you'll need to consider bandwidth and space. Security is also an essential issue to think about, and perhaps most importantly, you are going to need a platform that easily converts your content for viewing on a mobile device.

Although basic, I use WIX for mine and for my clients' sites because in addition to being as easy as using a word document with its drag and drop technology, it is constantly adding new apps and plugins – such as a members' area, or newsletter signup, or event management – which all improve your client's experience when visiting your site. It also has brilliant security and is bang up to date with data protection laws.

If you decide to go with a website developer, please consider working with someone who is going to take the time to understand who you are and what your business does. As a member of several Facebook Groups, a common complaint that I read about is from female entrepreneurs who find themselves being dictated to by designers on issues such as font and colour etc.

You must also ensure that the domain for your website is registered in *your* name, and not the name of the developer you work with. This is vital to be able to protect your copyright and intellectual property.

If you believe that your creative skills are lacking then some support can be valuable to kick-start your website. Just remember though that it is *your* website, and that you are paying the company to create *your* vision, not theirs.

Your logo

Your logo is one of the most intimate elements of your personal brand and my advice here is to be prepared for your ideas to change over time, and to not spend a huge amount of money with a professional designer until you are clear on your concept (which could take many months).

Most importantly, *you* must love your logo, because if you don't, you'll be draining yourself of enthusiasm and energy every time you look at it.

Here are some considerations:
- What is the personality of your business? Fun? Formal? Feminine?
- How sure are you that your product or service will stay the same for the next two/five/ten years?
- Check your audience avatar – keep your logo simple and easy for your clients to interpret ('clever' graphics and/or lots of text will look messy, and are expensive to print).
- Are you trading under your own name and should that be included in the logo?
- Do you already have favourite (business) colours? And what do those colours say about you?
- Do you have a favourite font? Is it easy to read in various sizes and colours?

One brilliant way of discovering what you want – or don't – is to go to Fiverr.com where you will find thousands of suppliers with thousands of ideas, all for a few dollars.

My current logo cost me just USD 20 to get sorted, but it took several months to refine the ideas. Remember, your logo represents you and your business, and it's vital that *you feel comfortable* with what you have before paying for your business cards and other marketing graphics.

Remember too that from now on, all your marketing must be aligned with what is on your website. Your clients and first-time site visitors need to get the same 'feeling' wherever they find you online.

Add your logo to your style guide (as above) and include variations such as colour or size to ensure consistency across all your social media. Your style guide will also make life a lot easier when you're creating new graphics or even get to the point where you ask someone else to take on the work, minimising the potential for mistakes which could damage your brand.

Your profile picture

In the world of personal branding, consistency is fundamental and your profile picture or photograph will likely be the first thing that people see when they search for you, so make sure that you have the same profile picture across all your social media accounts (no children, no pets, no holidays).

Think about the type of image you want to promote and get a photograph that matches. Don't worry if you don't want to justify paying a professional photographer for a full-on shoot just now. Even mobile 'phones can take a good quality picture these days, and you might also consider getting a passport-type (head shot) photograph done with you smiling. Just so long as it's digital, you'll be able to upload it easily.

Also think about the background and what is directly behind you– inside is better (maybe your office space or a conference room?). Depending on the sector you're working in I would lean towards a more formal setting (no beaches, restaurants full of people, gardens etc.).

#Hashtags

Hashtags are a really easy way of allowing your potential clients to find you on all social media platforms as well as internet search engines. They also allow you to promote and market your business very effectively by highlighting single key words or a frequently used phrase.

By searching for #FabulousFeelgoodFriday for example, you'll find me easily, even if you don't know which social media platform I'm using. You could also check out the results you get when you type *#LoveMyGarden* on Twitter, or *#Marketing* on Facebook, or indeed any other business sector, country, or interest you may have.

By adding hashtags to all your posts you'll help your clients access the information they need quickly. Simply use the hashtag character - # - with two or three of your key words (no spaces between the words) as demonstrated above.

Just a couple of words of caution. Don't go overboard as some social media platforms may penalise you by showing your posts to less people. Three hashtags in every post are a happy medium and will also encourage you to focus on your most important key words.

Creating Graphics and Headers

You are going to need to have 'Headers' on each of your profiles and not only are they different sizes on every platform, they sometimes change size as well. There are several fabulous free and easy options for you to create your images with pre-set templates, and by far my favourite is 'Canva'.

In an age where we are increasingly using our mobile 'phones to view social media content, you must also consider the size of your graphics (I'm talking pixels and megabytes). If they are too big and take too long to load, your client isn't going to wait patiently for your beautiful images to appear. If you're a windows user, the 'paint' programme is great for decreasing the size of your marketing graphics (and you can take similar action by using Canva).

Where should you show up?

The first two platforms we are going to look at are Facebook and LinkedIn. According to statistics women tend to network more on Facebook and men lean towards LinkedIn. From a professional perspective I would suggest that you should have a profile on both those platforms at a minimum.

Facebook

Clearly Facebook is doing something right, because despite all the negative press it has received about what happens with the data it collects from you, it continues to be THE most popular social media platform.

According to research compiled by the social media experts 'SmartInsights', 79 per cent of adults online have Facebook account, as compared with Instagram, Pinterest, LinkedIn and Twitter, for which the percentages of adults online range 'only' between 24 and 32 per cent.

From your perspective as an entrepreneur, Facebook's current challenge is to make space for the growing number of businesses who use it, and you will find them constantly pushing you to advertise. BUT, businesses who advertise also find themselves fighting for space in their potential client's newsfeed and you are going to have to be creative with how you use it. More of that a little later.

Before you begin any sort of marketing on Facebook, check your privacy settings to ensure that no information about you is being shared without you knowing about it. Whilst all social media platforms have a legal obligation to keep your data safe, you must take steps to do what you can to protect your profile and your content.

Crucially, please make sure that people cannot 'tag' you without your permission (also check the facial recognition feature), and if you want to keep tight control over what appears on your timeline, change the setting that allows others to post to your 'wall'.

Even the most well-meaning friends may be tempted to post a photograph from a birthday party or holiday in which they tag you, and whilst you may decide to allow some insights into your private life, you don't want your image to be irrevocably damaged because you were seen to have had one too many glasses of champagne, leering at the camera and sitting on a friend's lap!

Also check your profile settings and change what others can see if they are *not* connected with you. Facebook gives you a range of options spanning from 'public' to 'only me' (you) and as it continues to develop its security preferences I would recommend that you re-check your settings on a regular (monthly) basis.

Putting all of your contacts into lists (see the video on your downloads page) is a great feature on Facebook which gives you yet more control over who sees what you post, and also allows you to target specific groups.

For example, you could create a list called 'business' for your clients with whom you are connected so that you can post information relevant to them. Be aware however that if you select a specific audience on a post, those reading it will not be able to share it further.

On the subject of friend requests, if you receive a request from someone with no photograph and you don't know them, I would suggest deleting it (on all the platforms). If you get requests from people with the status of widower, or army general or similar, who show just two or three photographs of themselves or their children (grandchildren), they are usually spam and should be deleted.

Remember that if someone really wants to get in touch with you they can send you a message – and even then you'll have the option of accepting or rejecting it so that they will never know whether you saw it or not. Facebook allows you to block anyone you want to.

Do not use your Facebook login details (or Google for that matter) for other programmes/online tools even if it seems faster than creating yet another password. Doing so merely increases the amount of data that Facebook and others can collect from you.

By the same token, keep away from Facebook apps that require access to your online profile, for example those offering to show you what you would look like if you were a movie star, or offering to analyse your personality traits.

Because the focus of Facebook is to connect people *socially*, I would suggest that you don't make your entire employment/ education history available for everyone to see, but DO put your professional title with your name for everyone to see underneath your profile picture, and remember to connect your business page and/or website there too.

How should you use Facebook for your business?

Facebook is the biggest B2C space, but as previously mentioned, the fight for your attention in the newsfeed is getting stronger so you will have to get creative. You should consider your business page as a brochure for your products and services.

Your header reflects your brand, and I used Canva to create my Facebook version:

GwynethEL
Personal Branding Strategist

Nail Your Personal Brand and Market Yourself Magnificently

www.FeelgoodCoachingAndConsulting.Com

Pre-order my book today using the sign up button below and grab some great bonuses

If you want to provide value to your followers and encourage them to engage in a conversation, then consider setting up a group. Decide upon its purpose, for example a learning group where you hold a challenge or other online learning, and how you want your members to interact and/or benefit.

Carol Standing at Accordant Partners has successfully developed and managed clubs both online and offline, and has this advice:

"As a business owner one of the most valuable things that you can have is an ongoing relationship with your prospects and customers, allowing them to get to know, like and trust you. Facebook groups are the prefect mechanism for this.

There are four tips on how to ensure your group runs well:

1. Give your group a clear purpose so you attract the right members. You can then reflect this in the name that you choose and the content that you add to the 'About' section. Ask potential members qualifying questions before you approve their membership.

2. Set out guidelines so that your members are clear on what is and isn't acceptable, and make sure that the conversations occurring in your group are valuable to everyone. If possible, appoint a strong community manager who is regularly in the group, not only contributing but also moderating. That way, any conversation that is causing disruption can be dealt with at an early stage rather than 450 comments later!

3. Ensure that the content you're posting, both text and images, matches your brand. This will help your content to stand out and subtly reinforce your brand to the group members.

4. Welcome new members where possible. Most people will appreciate a personal mention and will be encouraged to contribute more quickly if they feel that they belong."

From your perspective, it will be worth your while to join groups of interest so that you can make new contacts online (more of that in Chapter 12 on networking).

One of Facebook's best features that won't change substantially (at least not negatively) is its ability for you to broadcast live.

Any type of video where *you* have the main role is going to allow your audience to connect with you within a couple of seconds. As technology develops so our brains evolve to keep up, and one result of those changes is that our attention spans are becoming less and less. Whilst images on Facebook are great, video in the form of going 'live' comes out on top because you can get your message across very quickly.

You can easily set up a webinar in your Facebook Group in the form of a live event, and it will cost you nothing. And after you have finished the live stream you can download your video and embed it on your website, or send a link to your email list.

There's a lot more to be said on the subject of video and live broadcasts, and Chapter 11 is dedicated to teaching you how you can get over yourself to be able to be a pro on camera.

Before we move on, be aware that Facebook's algorithms change on a regular basis, and I am not going to make the mistake of trying to predict what they will be in six months or a year.

The one thing I can tell you with certainty however, is that Facebook will never want you to send its users offsite (unless it's another site owned by Facebook). It doesn't want you to post links to videos on YouTube, and it doesn't want you to include URLs to your website within a post (put external links in to the 'comments' instead).

Facebook has a wide variety of tools – for example scheduling posts or adding captions to videos – to encourage you to use it for everything.

LinkedIn – a Man's World?

LinkedIn is *the* B2B space on the internet and the company is working quickly to improve how you can connect with others for business. Hootsuite – one of the social media marketing scheduling software programmes – says that with the number of users exceeding 500 million, more than one quarter of those logon and engage with the site's content on a monthly basis.

Another fact worth knowing is that 70 per cent of *active* LinkedIn users are outside of the US – something to bear in mind when you're working on your marketing plan.

Although a lot of statistics for demographics such as age and location may change, one thing is for sure: LinkedIn is more of a man's world. Expanded Ramblings tells us that 56 per cent of users are male and 44 per cent female (http://expandedramblings.com).

Remember too that social media platforms are full of algorithms helping you to find what you want, and on LinkedIn in particular you should be including lots of sector-specific and expertise-relevant key words (and hashtags) in your profile so that your ideal clients can find YOU easily too. With more than 15 million profile views *each day*, you would be daft to let this fabulous resource go to waste.

As is the case with Facebook, and before you start marketing and networking in a big way on LinkedIn, check (and change if necessary) your privacy and other settings and decide how much information you want people to see when they find you and/or want to connect with you.

A couple of great privacy settings features on LinkedIn are that you can choose whether your profile should be available to people *not registered* with them, and you can also set criteria for who you allow to send you a connection request.

There is nothing more off-putting than a profile that doesn't have a photograph, so if it isn't there yet, go and do it now. As I've already said, if someone sends me a connection request but all I can see is a logo, or even worse, nothing, I automatically delete it, and I know that a lot of others do the same.

More importantly though, LinkedIn says that having a profile photograph will get you 21 times more views than if you don't, and that could make the difference between you making a connection, or getting a contract, and not.

Not to be out-done by other social media platforms, LinkedIn also allows you to upload video directly to your posts and at the time of writing has begun to roll out the ability to broadcast live (in the same way that Facebook does). Watch this space.

Be 'client facing'

You have already worked out exactly who you want to work with, which sector and which type of company or person, and everything you write in your LinkedIn profile must be aimed at the person you are talking to.

Check out other people's profiles and you will see a lot of boring lists. You are so much more than a list of your skills and your elevator pitch that you created in Chapter 9 is going to form the basis of your profile. Be specific about the results you provide. If you're too general you will have put yourself in the 'generic' pot with thousands and thousands of others. You're better than that.

Your headline

If you have a university degree and/or you're allowed to put letters after your name, do so. It's not something that is usually done in the UK, but you don't know who is looking at your profile.

Gwyneth Letherbarrow MBA

Helping You to Nail Your Personal Brand so That You Turn Your Passion to Profit | Speaker | Author

gwyneth@feelgoodcoachingandconsulting.com

As you can also see, as a business owner, I have chosen to use the headline to describe the result that I deliver. What problems do *you* solve? Which results do *you* deliver? Don't waste that precious space with a generic title. Titles don't create emotional hooks. Talking about results does.

Scroll through the posts on LinkedIn and see what other people are using. You'll soon get a feel for what you like and what you don't like.

Your summary

Your elevator pitch is going to be your starting point for the summary and you will also be adding in a few more details. Write as though you were talking to a friend and match your language (key words) to the sector that you want to work in. Including key words will help the LinkedIn algorithm to make sure you appear in the right places as it is trawling through its records to provide search results for those looking.

For example, if you are working with scientists, your language is likely to be more technical and formal. If you are looking for work or business in the marketing or PR sectors, your language will probably be more straightforward and informal. Don't use jargon unless you are sure that everyone in your industry (and those looking at your profile) will understand it.

Pick what you consider to be the three most significant skills that you have for the work that you want to do and describe how and why they are relevant. Again, if you're not sure about how to start, go through some other LinkedIn profiles that you like and see what people are writing.

Your experience
At a minimum, upload everything that is relevant to your future goals. Don't list ! Your aim here is to stand out.

Include some achievements that demonstrate how brilliant you are. You could talk about setting up new systems, or developing software programmes, or effectively using resources, and mention what the impact was – it doesn't have to be something spectacular (although of course if it was then definitely put it in), but it does need to have made a positive difference to those you were working with. Ask yourself the question 'so what' for each item you include.

Education
Some people want to know that you finished compulsory education which is why I would suggest you include it, together with your later studies (not earlier).

Volunteer experience

LinkedIn encourages you to put something in this section, but it's entirely up to you.

Skills and endorsements

You have full control over what appears here. LinkedIn will send suggestions to your contacts based upon the key words in your profile/career history, and this is why it's important to stick to including information that is relevant to your future goals.

If you have been endorsed for something that you don't think is appropriate, simply delete it. And then take a look at your profile and work out why LinkedIn thought it would be useful to ask your contacts to endorse you.

If you get an endorsement, it's quite nice to return the favour. Although they're not written recommendations, they are still social proof, and they could make a difference to your network and your success.

Recommendations

These can be very powerful – but don't expect your contacts to be showering you with praise. ASK! LinkedIn provides you with a link to send to the person from whom you want a recommendation, and they can then post directly to your time line.

Give the person that you are asking a few questions to answer, because it will be much easier than simply asking them to write just anything. For example "could you please highlight how I contributed to xyz" or "could you please highlight my marketing skills and how they helped you win new business".

Accomplishments

Add languages only if you feel comfortable talking/working with them. A basic knowledge of a language may or may not be of benefit and I would suggest caution when telling others if you wouldn't be prepared to have a conversation (in that language). This is the part of your profile where you can include additional qualifications (keep them relevant) and information on any publications you have written.

Your Groups and Who You Follow

Be aware that people will judge you on this information too. That's not to say that you shouldn't belong to groups and/or follow people on LinkedIn, but remember to adjust your profile settings if you don't want others to see that information.

Your Profile

Having a completed profile will make a difference to how many times LinkedIn shows your posts in the newsfeed or includes you in search results. Complete every section on your profile to the extent possible, including the sector or industry that you work in (or want to work in), and the country or area where you live and work.

LinkedIn will prompt you and remind you frequently if you have left a section empty.

How should you use LinkedIn for your business?

Make connections

LinkedIn will frequently give you suggestions about who to connect with and you must decide how comfortable you are about connecting with people you don't know.

If they are in your sector/industry and you would like to add them to your network, write a short message with the connection request, for example "I saw that you belong to the group/work in the same sector/work with some of my contacts, and wondered whether you would like to connect here".

A gentle way of making new connections on LinkedIn is to join groups which share your interests, and to begin commenting on posts. Simple comments such as 'great article, thank you' or 'thanks for sharing' are easy to write (make sure you've read the article in question). Take it one step at a time.

Be consistent

That doesn't mean that you have to post daily or even weekly, but we are creatures of routine and habit, so decide on the frequency of your posts and stick to it. If you have a weekly or monthly blog, share it on LinkedIn through its 'Pulse' feature.

If you are holding a webinar or you have a special offer, post it on LinkedIn. Yes, it's male-dominated, but you just never know whether your ideal client or customer has been watching and waiting for this fabulous opportunity you have just presented. We are all human after all.

LinkedIn offers a premium service which allows you to see the names of everyone who has been checking your profile, but as a solopreneur I don't see the value in paying the extra money. Depending on your services and/or products, you may disagree.

Twitter

To tweet or not to tweet, that is the question. Having worked in different parts of Europe for many years, the feedback I have had from clients on the subject of Twitter is that it's for the rich and famous. OK – so what if you want to work with someone who is rich and famous you may ask?

Twitter has struggled to grow its number of users significantly since the beginning of 2016, and WhatsApp and Facebook remain stark competitors (www.statista.com). When looked at in isolation however, its user numbers in the UK have increased steadily during recent years, and that trend is predicted to continue.

Whether you decide to use it or not therefore will very much depend upon where you believe your target market to be, and Twitter is still the number two B2C marketing platform after Facebook.

Photograph – you know this already. Use the same photograph across all your social media platforms. Also create a header graphic that matches your branding and marketing elsewhere online.

Because the majority of people don't spend hours trawling through posts on Twitter, you must use hashtags if you want to attract the attention of potential clients and you should include them in your short profile as well.

I have worked with some fabulous mentors to learn about social media, and none of them ever gave the same advice about the number of times I should be tweeting. Much will depend upon your audience and where they're located, so do your research before you embark on a campaign that yields little or no results.

Remember to check the analysis and insights about the number of impressions that your posts receive that Twitter provides on a regular basis so that you can adapt your content according to what works best.

Instagram

If you and your client base love visuals, this is the place for you. Images always attract more attention than sentences of text, and Instagram is continuously developing its mobile app to make it easier for you to post photographs and short videos on the move.

It definitely isn't the place for you to hold meaningful conversations with your followers – they're there for the pictures – and so it's important to include links back to your website and other contact details within your profile. Having said that, if you receive comments on your posts, always respond. Followers are fickle and if you ignore them completely you'll lose them.

Keep your hashtags on Instagram to a maximum of three and make sure that they're relevant to your topic.

Post your holiday photographs when you're home again so as not to invite burglars (to your home or indeed your office if you have one).

As with all other marketing, how your audience feels when it sees your posts will be key to your success. I think that there's an exciting energy around Instagram that makes Facebook feel like a tank in comparison, and whilst it attracts a lot of younger users, you'll find that it brings out the creativity in everyone.

Google Plus

This is a tricky one and from my experience people either love or hate Google Plus. Before you decide to discount this section however, please remember that Google is a major player in all things internet. Amongst others, it owns YouTube, Google Maps and AdSense (which allows others to advertise on your sites bringing you extra income).

At a minimum you should create a Google Plus page for your business and get it verified so that you appear on Google Maps. You can then upload information about your website, opening hours, contact details etc., which will give you increased visibility if someone searches for your services.

Remember to create a header graphic and to upload your photograph. You never know who is going to find you.

The only time I post to Google Plus is when I publish my weekly vlog on YouTube, and I have never had any direct interaction. Since I began doing so however, my website traffic has increased, so clearly there is some good being done. But I also know that its algorithms are set up in such a way that if you're not on their platform, you will receive less exposure elsewhere.

If you want to find out more about the power of Google, its 'Digital Garage' is the best place to start:
https://learndigital.withgoogle.com/digitalgarage/

Pinterest

Pinterest is very different to the other social media platforms in that its users ie., your followers or fans use it specifically to look for ideas – and according to statistics they will stay on the site for an average of 14 minutes pinning pictures every time they login!

Pinterest can also boast that "87% of Pinners have purchased a product because of Pinterest".
https://blog.hootsuite.com/pinterest-statistics-for-business/

As with everything else, before you begin posting content ensure that your business profile is complete with your photograph and other relevant (contact) information. You also have the option of verifying your website which will give you added credibility as a business person. DO use the business profile option so that you have access to the valuable insights, analytics and other benefits that Pinterest provides.

Pinterest requires strategy and planning, so work out what it is that you want to achieve before you start pinning. You may decide to create Pin Boards with the titles of all your business keywords (potentially great for SEO).

If you want to start off by creating your own content to build your authority and demonstrate your expertise, infographics are a great way of getting the attention of potential clients (use www.canva.com to create them within minutes).

As was the case with Twitter, those I learned from had varying opinions on how to approach Pinterest. If you decide that this platform is for you, please take the time to find out what you feel comfortable with and then stick to it. Remember, consistency is key, and Pinterest's 'board' concept has the ability to spread your message to those who are interested very quickly.

Summary

So there you have six of the top players for social media where you can create a strategy without having to go too far out your comfort zone. If it all seems like too much to take in, and as I mentioned at the beginning of the chapter, it will be well worth your while researching where your audience hangs out, and then focusing on one or two of the options.

There are some fabulous teachers and short courses on social media out there and I have included some suggestions in the resources section at the end of the book. But if you're the type of person who wants to focus their efforts on other things, there are also plenty of freelancers who will happily do your social media for you. Just remember to agree on your outcomes in advance, check in with them regularly, and *never* take your eye off the ball.

Chapter 11 ~ Video

"Video informs and entertains people, good or bad, today most people prefer to watch a video than read a page of text." -
Lisa Lubin

In this chapter I'm going to introduce you to the basics of recording video for business use, and we'll also look at your options for using it on social media.

The use of video for business is growing faster than any other technology, and although it will never replace our *in-person* communications, it has got to be better than the dreadful alternatives such as dreary emails and messaging services which, despite the use of symbols and emojis, have caused more disagreements in business than I could possibly count.

Video is a fantastic option to market to your potential audience because it allows you to get your personality across in an instant. Within just a few seconds you can make that all-important emotional connection with those watching, by 'showing' your enthusiasm and passion for your service or product.

From an advertising perspective, whilst long 'copy' can be useful for giving details, technology has had a negative impact on our attention spans, and we want the answers NOW (and don't necessarily want to be reading a load of words to find out what it is we supposedly can't live without any more).

Be kind to yourself if you have never done video before, because seeing yourself on film for the first time could be a shock.

Whenever you look at yourself in a mirror, you are seeing a *reflection* of your face and your brain is telling you what you look like, but when you see yourself on camera, you are seeing yourself as others see you.

And you know how people talk about putting on an extra 10 lbs as soon as they show up on screen? It's one of the reasons that so many immediately shy away from using this incredible resource.

Don't expect to become an expert overnight. Talking to the camera takes practise, and it might take a few dodgy recordings before you begin to feel even mildly comfortable with how you present yourself.

Your equipment

If you are just going to be using video for social media posts and short marketing videos, you can probably get away with using the camera on your mobile 'phone. You may however consider the purchase of two inexpensive items, namely a selfie-stick with a stand or tripod to hold your 'phone whilst recording, and a separate lapel microphone to plug into your 'phone and which clips onto your clothing. You can get both those items for under £25!

And if you don't like the walls of your home or office, you could also purchase a backdrop for around £20. You can find all the links on the Stepping Into You Downloads Page here: **http://bit.ly/SIY_The_Downloads**

Most computer operating systems include some sort of basic video editing software and there are hundreds of free Apps available to you. For my weekly vlogs and online programmes I started with Movie Maker (for Windows) and then moved over to CyberLink, both of which also allow music and captions to be added very easily.

Music

Adding music to your videos will give your finished product a professional touch although you must be sure to use it legally to avoid prosecution. You only need search for 'royalty free music' on the internet to find thousands of options, some of them requiring payment, and some not.

An annual subscription to a company such as Audioblocks provides you fabulous value in the form of unlimited downloads, and on the rare occasions when YouTube has told me that I was using music for which I had no licence, Audioblocks had it sorted within 24 hours (always in my favour).

So you see, starting out with video doesn't require an expensive outlay, and you can research more advanced (and more pricey) options as you learn about your own video recording needs.

Be a Pro on Video

Before we get onto the specific platforms, here are my five top tips to start you off on your video adventures (even if you're using a mobile 'phone!).

1. Preparation is everything

Is the video a vlog? Is the video for your website? Is the video marketing a product or service? Remember that regardless of which service or product you are selling, your clients are buying the way that *you* make them *feel*. How you present yourself matters! Decide on who you are talking to and what you want to achieve *before* you start recording. Also decide on which hashtags (keywords) you want to use (I'll go into more detail on this when we talk about YouTube).

2. Check how much of you is on camera

If you're filming a short message, make sure that you can see your face! Ideally your head and shoulders will be in the frame. If you're any further away you'll lose the connection to the person watching. After all, if you were speaking to someone in person, you wouldn't stand six feet away from them would you? If you're going to add captions to the finished product, move a little to the right or the left of the video area so that you don't end up with text covering your face.

3. SMILE at the beginning and the end of your video clip

This is one of the most useful tips I learned from the Pros, namely to smile for a couple of seconds at the beginning of the video clip, before you start speaking, and again at the end. It will make your editing much easier, AND you'll be able to use your smiling face as a thumbnail/cover (instead of you appearing with your mouth open or your eyes closed).

4.   Focus on the camera lens

Cameras are usually very small and looking at them is made more difficult because they are located in the frame of your 'phone or laptop which is usually dark. But you must make sure that you are looking at the camera on your 'phone or laptop, and not the screen. If you look at the screen the person watching will think that you're looking downwards and you'll lose the emotional connection.

Something I suggest to my clients which is easy and very effective, is to cut out a circle from a piece of paper, and then cut out a small circle in the centre of the larger circle. Stick it over the camera on your 'phone (or laptop or tablet or whatever) so that you have a larger surface on which to focus.

5.   Behave as if you were talking to your favourite client or customer (or friend)

Have you ever watched someone on screen who simply doesn't move? They just stand there talking with a monotone voice and you're bored after about 10 seconds. OK so it takes some practice, but imagine that you're talking to your most favourite client or customer, or even a friend).

If you're the type of person who gestures with their hands, then use them on camera as well.   By being as natural as possible you have a better chance of making that all important emotional connection.

Video on your website

What better way to greet people when they first visit your website than with a short video?

Think about the last time you went to a new town or shopping centre and had to find your way around. Given the choice, would you look at a map and spend time working out your route, or would you prefer to ask someone who knew the fastest way to get you to your destination?

A welcome video on your website can:

- Direct your visitor to the various pages of your website that you want to highlight.
- Inform your visitor of any free resources you have to download so that you get their email address for your mailing list.
- Encourage your visitor to sign up for a webinar or live event that they might otherwise not have known about.
- Help you to connect emotionally with your visitor instantaneously because you can more easily express your personality

Visitors to your website are more likely to watch your two or three-minute video to the end than they are to scroll up and down your page not knowing what they're looking for, which will get you a higher ranking on Google because they have spent a longer time on your website. (The less time someone spends on your site, the less popular you're going to be for Google).

Having watched your introductory video, your site visitor will remember you longer than if they had just had a quick browse – and if they liked what they saw they will return to find out more, allowing you to further build your relationship with them, albeit indirectly.

Another important consideration is the significant rise in the use of mobile devices to access the internet, because it is much easier to watch a video on a smart 'phone than to attempt to read pages of small writing until you finally find what you wanted (by which time the majority will have given up).

And if you're anything like me, and even though I've written this book, sometimes it is just easier to explain an idea or concept, or to describe your services and products, using the spoken word.

I speak from experience when I say that this is especially relevant if you have a high-end offer on your website, for example an online programme spanning several months. I found that when I added a video to the sales copy describing my 'Personal Branding Bootcamp', engagement increased markedly.

Video for your YouTube Channel

Hopefully by now you are beginning to understand how fabulous video can be for you and your business and having a YouTube channel opens up a whole new world because it's the platform that people visit to specifically watch videos.

YouTube is a science in itself and please don't be put off by terminology such as 'meta-tags' or video SEO. As with everything else, you don't need to be an expert to begin, and you'll find that once you get started you will quickly learn what you need.

I have used YouTube to find instructions on diverse topics such as how to use gel nail-varnish, as well as how to unblock my dishwasher. I think of YouTube as the video version of Encyclopaedia Britannica – it is truly fabulous.

Setting up your own YouTube channel is easy and as with everything else, you should get it connected and then verified with your website (so that you can use your business name). The YouTube help centre is extensive and you don't need me to go into details here.

Once you're ready to go, record a welcome video for your channel start page so that as is the case on your website (you've done your website welcome video already right … ?) visitors get to see your smiley face with a warm welcome when they arrive. Ask them to subscribe! They'll then receive a notification every time you upload new content.

Make your channel as easy as possible to navigate by creating playlists covering specific topics and post regularly. The jury is out – again - on how often you should post, and if you're just starting out, then a short video once a week is going to be fine. Remember to post valuable content because you are putting your personal brand out there and building important relationships with potential clients.

The Google brain (aka artificial intelligence) reads not only the words in the description you add to your video, but it can also listen in to what you're saying, so if you want to get noticed, include your key words as often as possible.

Before you upload your video to YouTube make sure that you have already given it a title and a description. YouTube wants you to send viewers to more videos, so including a link to another of your videos is an easy way of doing that.

And to make sure that you're maximising your potential to market your business it's also a good idea to also include a link to your website in the description box for the video, maybe to your blog, or to the sign-up page for your mailing list.

YouTube allows you to include your key words separately, and also allows you to immediately share your video across a broad number of social media platforms.

You can use it to livestream for webinars, and you have the choice of placing limits on who sees your videos. For example, if you have an online programme that is only available to paying clients, you would check 'unlisted' on your video so that only people with the link can find it.

YouTube allows you to upload a video to your channel and then embed it into your website in the blink of an eye – and that's the facility I use for all the videos on my website. Of course there are other programmes available for you to host your videos, but none so powerful and with as much exposure as YouTube.

You may have heard about YouTubers earning millions … it confused me for a while because I didn't see anyone asking for money to watch the videos. It's all down to advertising and affiliate marketing! Although you can sign up to allow advertising on your channel – and you get to choose what that advertising looks like - you must have had 10,000 views before YouTube will start placing ads with you.

So there you have it. YouTube presents a huge opportunity to promote your personal brand and business, and its benefits will far outweigh any cringeworthy moments you have when you record your first video.

Video for Facebook Live

Facebook and Google/YouTube are huge rivals, which is one of the reasons that Facebook wants you to do everything 'video' directly with them. It can be a pain if you're having to upload content twice over (first on YouTube and then on Facebook), and you may even decide that life is simply too short to be faffing around. But the Facebook Live option is just fabulous!

Your followers will love to know what you're up to and I've had a particularly high number of video views when I've streamed from events such as an awards ceremony, or at a conference with lots of hustle and bustle. What is even better however is that you can use it in a closed group for a webinar, or for a question and answer session with your clients.

As with everything else, preparation is key, and it is good practice to let your followers know well in advance that you are going to be streaming live. Don't just go live for the sake of it, be clear on the purpose of your livestream, which messages you want to get across, whether you want to include a call to action, and how long you are going to be live for.

Once you have completed your live stream, make sure to click on the 'post to Facebook' button that will come up on the screen so that your followers can view the video after it has finished. You'll also be able to download it as an MP4 file, upload it on to YouTube, and embed it on your website.

Captions

I'm really doing my best to be as objective and informative about what I'm sharing with you here, and as you will have seen, a lot of my advice is based upon personal experience as well as the experience of my clients. But when it comes to captions, the differences in opinion are extreme.

Fact: You never know which device someone is using when they watch your videos (although your insights and analytics will reveal that information to you fairly quickly once you start posting).

Fact: You don't know whether they are going to be watching with the sound on or off and/or whether they have their headphones plugged in to listen.

Fact: Visitors to YouTube go there to watch videos and they will have their sound turned on (at least this is what YouTube tells you). You won't see too many captions or script there.

And thereafter it all gets very murky.

On Facebook, users have the option to play videos automatically, with or without sound, as they are scrolling through their newsfeed. Some social media experts argue that you must have the accompanying captions on all your videos, and Facebook gives you the ability to automatically generate the relevant text. The voice recognition tool is lumpy though, especially if you're not a native English speaker. No doubt it will improve over time …

The other school of thought says that if someone is interested in watching your video ie., if it's someone who follows you or who is attracted by the title and text in your post, then they *will* turn up the sound.

You're going to have to decide this one for yourself by closely monitoring the number and length of views of your videos.

If you decide that you want to upload captions, then I will recommend that you use a professional company such as Rev.Com which provides incredible value and a number of options for file format, *and* it allows you to easily edit your text (I didn't realise how often I said 'gonna' instead of 'going to' until I started doing video) before you download the final file.

Summary

Video is fabulous and so are you – it's the perfect match.

Chapter 12 ~ Networking

"It occurs to me that our survival may depend upon our talking to one another." —
Dan Simmons

If you want to take a break, do it now because when it comes to networking, if that little voice in your head has begun to quieten down during the previous chapters, it could well get much louder again right now.

Networking used to scare the living daylights out of me, and even these days I sometimes ask myself what gives me the right to be talking to you and others ... Who am I to be giving advice on your personal brand and marketing your business ...?

You will have heard all sorts of suggestions and plans about how to best network, meet new people and make business contacts, but the truth of it is that you just have to be *you*. And remember that every time you break the ice and say hello, the person you are speaking to is probably going to be hugely relieved that you took the initiative.

In this chapter I'm going to show you how to network online and offline, and also how to use stealth networking so that the people you're communicating with don't even realise it. OK so you might think that's a bit sneaky, but it can be incredibly effective.

Just always remember to be interested in the conversations you're having. Don't fake it. If you come from a place of need, ie., you're desperate for new clients, your contacts will sense it. Anyway, you know by now that you have a fabulous personal brand, and you know that there are people out there who will benefit from your services or products.

Why don't we like talking to strangers?

Go on, just blame your parents again, and think of all the times they told you to never talk to strangers. As children it is drummed into us that we should keep away from adults we don't know for all the right reasons.

And then you're grown up and marketing your fabulous products or services, and the only way that your business will grow is if you can strike up a conversation with someone you don't know. It goes against every cell in your body.

Building empathy means opening up to others, which in turn makes you feel vulnerable. But you don't have to start off by telling a stranger your entire life story, you just have to find out where the common denominators are.

One of the reasons that you're still reading this book is that I am sharing real-life examples of mistakes that I have made, as well as stories of success from my clients, because I want you to know that I get it. I've done what you're doing, and I know it's not always a bed of roses. If we were to meet up for a coffee next week we could probably speak for several hours.

In my workshops I include an exercise on how to start a conversation with a stranger, and although participants are reluctant at first (boy oh boy if looks could kill), when those first few words have been spoken, they become so engrossed that they don't want to stop talking.

A lifelong business partnership or friendship can begin with simple words such as 'what brings you here today?', or 'what was the traffic like getting here?', or even 'I love your shoes, are they Jimmy Choo's?'.

Online

So how on earth are you supposed to strike up a conversation with someone online, someone who you may not even be connected with, let alone know them in real life?

It's simple.

You do it by joining groups and following other business pages. Facebook and LinkedIn are awash with groups on a vast array of topics and interests. Do your research and have a look around. Put your business keywords into the search box for groups and see what comes up.

Do you want to network with people close to where you live? Search for online groups that contain the name of your town. Do you only want to network with women? There are thousands of women-only groups online.
Look for groups where there is a good level of conversation or

engagement. You'll find that some of them are so huge that they are of no benefit to anyone. Pay attention to how you *feel* when you're reading the description of the page or group. Even if you join and subsequently find out that it isn't the right place for you to be, you can always leave.

An important factor about Facebook groups in particular is that they can provide a fabulous sense of community, and as a solopreneur it will be great to meet others who understand where you're coming from. You could start right now by joining the 'Stepping into You' Facebook group where you'll get to see everything I write about in this book put into action.

You don't have to go in of these groups all guns blazing. Start off by reading what others are saying. If someone is asking a question and you know the answer, leave a comment. Don't be shy, because if they have asked the question then it means that they are looking for help. Don't assume that everyone in your groups knows everything about everything. It simply isn't true.

One thing I learned from one of my coaches and mentors, Veronica Pullen, the Social Marketing Queen, was that you should comment at least 10 times on others' questions or problems, before asking for input on your own.

When you first get to join a group, don't ever start off by plugging your business unless the community guidelines specifically state that that is what you should do. Even then, I'd suggest that you wait a couple of weeks to see what other members are talking about before you write your 'hello and lovely to be here' message.

Networking on LinkedIn is more formal and with engagement and conversation, it doesn't even come close to Facebook. You'll see popular posts with hundreds of comments, but frequently the author hasn't responded to any of them.

LinkedIn's networking opportunities are more passive in that its algorithm allows your posts to be circulated to a much wider audience than Facebook. We already talked about how to create your profile on LinkedIn, and by using key words and hashtags in your posts (and videos) you are more likely to get noticed by the people you want to notice you.

My experience has been that if someone is interested in one of your posts they will look at your profile, and if they still think you have something worth saying they'll send you a connection request – and that is where the conversation usually starts.

Another way that I have networked on LinkedIn was to send a personal message to each of my contacts (the majority of whom I have never met in person) asking them if they wanted my cheat sheet on staff engagement. Two-thirds of them said yes – most people love free stuff, especially if it means they don't have to sign up to yet another mailing list – which meant that I was able to keep the conversation going.

The other major platforms – Google+, Twitter, Instagram and Pinterest don't particularly lend themselves to deep and meaningful conversations. As previously mentioned though, if someone does take the time to comment on one of your posts, always respond, even if it's a simple 'thank you'.

No-one likes a hard sell, and remember that even if the people you are talking to online don't want to buy from you, they have a stack of friends and colleagues who may want what you offer.

Stay aligned with your values and your business, and people will love your authenticity.

By continuing to build your online relationships, you could be setting yourself up for some fabulous referrals. And believe me, those are the best sort of business leads you could hope for.

Offline

Keeping your personal brand strong online is straightforward once you have all your logos, colours and content sorted. Offline requires more work, because as a solopreneur you will find yourself networking all the time.

Remember that we judge each other within just a few seconds of first sight, so don't be tempted to walk to the corner shop for some milk in your comfortable tracksuit without having brushed your hair properly. You can bet that you will bump into someone you know, and then feel as though you want to crawl into a hole.

Don't stick to just business networking events. Yes, they can be useful, and it's great to be connected with people in your local community, but the downside is that everyone wants to sell something. I have been to events enticed by promises of breakthroughs and new learning, and have then spent six or seven hours listening to a sales pitch. Not great.

There are thousands of opportunities to network with like-minded solopreneurs, business owners, photography fans, authors, film fanatics, football fans … You name it, there's probably an event near to you that covers the topic that appeals to you.

Sign up to events that interest you *personally,* because it is precisely on those occasions that you are more likely to meet people with similar values who you really like. When you meet people socially there is less pressure to impress, and whilst I'm not suggesting for one moment that you should leave your personal brand at home, creating empathy is going to be much easier if you're operating on a personal level.

An easy way to find out what is going on around you is to type the name of your hobby (or business interest) and the name of your town (or wherever you want to go) into your search engine and see what comes up. Eventbrite is a popular platform and has thousands of suggestions all over the world, and local news sites will also list events and meetings close by.

If you're nervous about going to an event on your own, think carefully about whether you really want to take a friend with you because there's a danger that you will spend most of your time talking to each other. One way of easing yourself into networking with strangers is to volunteer for a cause important to you.

Do whatever you can to get comfortable with introducing yourself (you already have a fabulous elevator pitch). Like I said, you don't have to tell them your life story as soon as you meet, and you don't need to be able to talk to them for hours on end. But you do need to be able to exchange pleasantries and have a short conversation without going into panic mode.

With practice you'll be introducing yourself as if you had been networking your entire life. And if you're still nervous, ask yourself this question: "what have I got to lose?"

Stealth Networking

Although stealth networking may sound a bit sneaky, it's actually very easy and can be incredibly effective. It's all about engaging with others who are already popular, because if they're good at online networking, chances are that they will have a great network offline too.

When you've joined a few groups on Facebook and LinkedIn, or you've decided who you want to follow on other platforms, watch to see which people get the most likes or comments. Then add your own comment, or answer the question posed for as many of their posts as possible without being weird. Get involved in the conversation and maintain a discreet presence.

Eventually you'll notice that you are getting more likes and comments on the things that you post, which means that others in the group are beginning to notice you. When that happens, you'll begin to get more profile visits and when that happens ... hey presto, you could have just landed yourself with a fabulous new client.

Stealth networking offline requires greater diplomacy and a lot of research. For example, if you provide services to people in the legal profession, consider what other types of services *they* need, such as an accountant, or even a dry cleaner!

Then next time you meet someone who is an accountant, don't immediately dismiss them, rather make the connection and remember to tell them that you work with people in the legal profession. They'll remember *you* for being interested in them as a human being, even though they weren't your ideal client, and when they're doing the next quarterly return for *their* clients and they're asked if they know someone who does what you do, they'll tell their clients about you.

The stealth networking approach takes time. It requires discretion, dedication and consistency, but it's a great way to raise your profile in a non-invasive and non-threatening way.

Summary

As with everything else, networking requires practice, and as long as you remain aligned and keep telling yourself that you have nothing to lose, you'll do brilliantly.

Part Five

THRIVE

Chapter 13 ~ Your Marketing Strategy

"Strategy is not the consequence of planning,
but the opposite; its starting point." -
Henry Mintzberg

This chapter sets out my framework of activities to help you focus on what you want to achieve. Keep things simple to begin with so that you have a good overview of what is working and what isn't.

You have defined your personal brand and you must now build your business by marketing yourself with confidence. You are ready to create a marketing strategy that is completely aligned with your values and the business of your future.

You have to trust that you have what it takes and remember that nothing you do will ever have been worthless. There is no 'one size fits all' because you provide something unique to your clients.

Begin by setting yourself a maximum of three goals for the year, and then work backwards, splitting your planning into quarterly and then monthly activities.

For each of your monthly plans you are going to focus on just one activity so that a) you give yourself a decent amount of time to gather insights and analytics and b) so that you can then adjust your activities during the following month accordingly, all the time keeping your eye on the bigger goals.

Focusing on one thing at a time is also a fantastic preventative measure if you are prone to procrastination and slipping into overwhelm.

Always remember your 'why', and always focus on how amazing you're going to feel when you have made it.

Align. Release. Trust. Transform. Thrive.

Get it out of your brain and onto paper

Whilst technology can help us manage our work more efficiently, every time you begin some new planning activities I would strongly encourage you to do it by hand to help your brain focus on your creativity and not worry about whether you are writing the letters on your laptop keyboard in the right order.

There are some fabulous notebooks out there, so buy a large one that makes your heart sing every time you look at it. It shouldn't be used for meeting notes or travel details or indeed anything else in it that is not marketing-related.

Your annual goals

Close your eyes and think about where you want to be 12 months from now. As mentioned above, I want you to first choose your overall goals and outcomes, and work backwards. You're going to have to trust me on this. You have a much better chance of succeeding doing it this way around, instead of focusing on the detail first and then hoping it takes you to where you want to be.

Here's a quick summary of how to use the SMART way to set goals.

Be *specific* – for example you may want to have increased your turnover by 10 or 50 or even 100 per cent, or maybe you want to be working with 10 private clients who match your ideal, five-start client avatar. Or maybe you want to be holding one successful workshop every month.

If you're using numbers in your goal they are going to be easily *measurable* – you are going to know whether you have hit your targets. If your goal is too vague, such as 'I want to be a successful business woman', you could find yourself changing the goalposts and never reaching your dream. How would you define success?

You also want your goals to be *achievable*. Make sure that you really want what you're planning and that your goals are aligned with your values.
Do you have the resources to get all the work done? Be *realistic*. If you have to depend on others, you could be left disappointed.

"A goal is a dream with a deadline" – Napoleon Hill, which is why all your planning should be *timebound*.
Don't rush this process, and don't set goals that you think you *should*. The work you have already done here has helped you to learn what is right by how you *feel* about something and not what you *think* about it.

And remember, even though I've told you to stick to your plan so that you allow yourself to see what works and what doesn't, nothing is ever written in stone. If you start to sense that something isn't *sitting comfortably* but you don't know what it is or why, step back and focus again on the feeling.

If it doesn't feel right, then pushing against that feeling and putting yourself under pressure to continue with the work will result in your negative and uncertain energy finding its way into what you're doing. It is imperative that you trust your gut, even if your logic is telling you something else.

Don't change who you are. If you need to, change the type of people you're working with, but always keep your business aligned with your personal brand.

Your core offer

Up until now we haven't talked in any great detail about your core offer and without knowing you (I hope that changes) it's impossible for me to give you advice on potential gaps, or indeed whether you are offering too much.
Just remember that your core offer is at the heart of your business and is likely to be your main source of income. It could come in the form of a high-ticket year-long mastermind or it may be a mid-priced seven-modules online bootcamp.

You may also have cheaper services or products (as well as a freebie to encourage others to sign up to your mailing list), and you might also have much more expensive things on offer, but they will all revolve around the essence of your *core* or *evergreen* product or service.

For example, the core product in my business is the 'Stepping into You Bootcamp' (online course). I then also have a shorter version called 'Stepping into You – The Basics', and I also offer a 1:1 Coaching Package 'Stepping into You Platinum' which runs for 12-months. And you are reading the most recent addition to my offer in the form of this book.

The marketing structure is the same for each. Its aim is to provide value and to build a relationship with a client, and what follows is the exact process that all my clients use.

1.   Start off with a value exchange tool, a freebie for someone to download in exchange for them giving you their name and email address (make sure that you and/or your mailing list provider are GDPR compliant). For example, you could offer a checklist, a short eBook or even a 20-minute call. Make it relevant and keep it simple.

The link to sign up can be placed on your website, on your Facebook business page, on your LinkedIn profile, on your YouTube channel description, in your email signature block, and wherever else you're showing up online.

2.   Once someone is on your mailing list, they will receive regular emails from you for example your blog or vlog, or practical tips, or additional free tools (templates etc).

3.   After five or six emails you then offer them a paid product or service, also known as a conversion tool. This could cost anywhere between £7 and £197.

4.   If they purchase the lower priced product or service, you can then continue marketing to them with the aim of getting them to

sign up for one of your other, more highly priced, services or products.

All the while you'll be keeping an eye on providing great value, and staying aligned with your annual goals. Once you have determined your three major goals for the next 12 months, you can move onto breaking down your activities into 90-day and 30-day segments.

Your 90-day marketing plan

By dividing your year into quarterly and monthly segments you are going to make life (and work) much easier for yourself.

One of the reasons that businesses fail is that they have great goals, but they have no strategy or structure that is going to lead them to success. You will know that if you have ever applied for a business loan or funding, the lending authority doesn't just want to know how much money you intend to make, but also what type of business you're in so that they can make a realistic risk assessment of your success.

'Fail to prepare and prepare to fail' – is one of the most valuable phrases you will ever hear. You must be able to track what is happening with your business so that you can adjust your activities if necessary, without endangering your annual goals.

Put time in your diary for every 90-day and 30-day planning session, and also set time aside for review. Yes, your day to day activities are important, but remember that you are the CEO of your business, and you must keep your eye on the big picture.

So – you know where you want to be in 12 months from now, and you're going to split your year into four quarters. Answer these questions:

- What has worked well up until now?
- What hasn't worked so well?
- Has your audience changed and either way, what does your five-star client look like (you know this already)?
- Which social media platform(s) are you going to focus on *(please don't try to do them all unless you're not sure and you want to get insights for a month or two to be able to then make a decision)*?
- What is your core product? Do you already have a product or service to be marketed or do you want to make changes?
- What is your marketing budget?
- How many hours are you going to dedicate to marketing your business each week?

Whenever you are deciding on your activities, begin by asking yourself the question 'what *could* I do' (this works in any language). Your brain will then help you to come up with a variety of ideas. Some of them will be brilliant, and some will not, but don't discount anything until you have taken each one through the SMART process.

If I'm working with a client I ask them to make a list of 30 things that they could do to take them closer to their goal. Why not try doing the same and see what happens. Also notice how you *feel* as you go through your ideas. What is your body telling you?

The more time you spend planning, the easier it will be to take action, and the faster you'll succeed. Whenever you plan your 90-day segments, wait a day or two and then go back to them and see whether they still feel right. If they don't, change them.

Work backwards

Yep, you read that correctly. Start off with planning your fourth quarter (I'll call it Q4 from now on). Look at your annual goals and ask yourself what would have to happen in those last few months to get you the results you want.

Clearly you would not leave all your marketing activities until Q4 because people don't usually decide to invest thousands of pounds in a product or service as a result of getting a few emails from you or seeing one or two of your posts on Facebook.

Brainstorm the types of activities that would help your (potential) clients make the decision to invest with you or increase their spend, or whatever else it is you want them to do.

Regardless of which sector you're in, events are great for boosting your clients' commitment because they allow personal interaction. For example, if you're in retail you could arrange an open day and invite your clients to come and sample your wares.

One of my clients operates a retail business online and invited everyone on her mailing list to come and visit her at the product storage location. Her sales numbers went through the roof, all for the cost of an email, a few glasses of prosecco and some snacks.

When you've worked out your activities for Q4, move back another step into Q3. That will be where you begin your marketing in earnest for your end of year event, or the activity you have chosen. Your marketing could involve the purchase of a lower priced product, or an opportunity to win a VIP invitation or additional bonus.

Another client sent out VIP invitations to her coaching database for an upcoming event and included a pen with a motivational quote written on it. She had a very fast uptake on her offer. The rule of reciprocation (providing a freebie and getting something in return) is a powerful tool if you want to encourage your clients to commit. "Each of us has been taught to live up to the rule, and each of us knows the social sanctions and derision applied to anyone who violates it" (Cialdini, R. B. (2009) "Influence").

After you're clear on Q3, move back another step into Q2. Here you're potentially going to be wanting to build your email list by offering free downloads, webinars, and other valuable content to position yourself as the expert in your sector/region.

Then move back another step into Q1. This is when you will be asking your Facebook followers (or group) to take part in surveys telling you what their biggest headaches are so that you can provide relevant marketing content to them.

You may still be deciding about where you want to focus your online marketing efforts. Regardless of which social media platforms you choose, you want to engage with your audience as much as you can and build a solid client relationship.

OK so that's just a very simple outline describing how you could break down your 90-day plans. By working out what needs to happen in each quarter you can set 90-day *goals* as well.

Working backwards acts as a failsafe to ensure that you keep your eye on the big dreams, without getting bogged down and lost in the details and irritations of daily life.

Always review your achievements at the end of those 90-days and again answer some questions that you should now know:

- What went well?
- What didn't go well?
- What *could* I do differently next time – and only then decide on what you *will* do.

Feel your way through the answers.

To make things easy for you, I'm giving you access to a copy of one of my 90-day and 30-day marketing plan templates (on the Stepping into You downloads webpage) which include examples of how to complete each of the columns on them. Remember, use a pen (or pencil) and paper for your planning because it will help you feel better about making changes.

Your 30-day marketing plan

Let's assume then that you are clear on your annual and 90-day goals. You have the bones of your marketing plan and you need to give it some substance. Obviously you also want to be earning some money and your 30-day plans are going to help you do precisely that, whilst all the time contributing to your end of year goals.

For each of your 30-day marketing plans , focus on *one* idea, which means that for your 90-day plan you'll have a total of *three* ideas to work on. Remember to check that your plans are SMART.

For example, let's say you want to start building your email list and that within the next 30 days you want to have 200 new sign-ups.

You could focus your marketing on encouraging your ideal clients on Facebook and Pinterest to sign up for a free download, such as 'three tips on how to look like a pro on video'. The follow-up email sequence for that type of offer would include additional advice on how to talk to the camera and an invitation to join your Facebook Group.

In the same or following month you would want to be moving those new email clients towards your conversion tool (low cost) and which could be a short sequence of videos with a couple of worksheets showing the client how to create a marketing video and upload it on to YouTube.

In month three you would then move on to more advice about speaking in public and presenting with confidence, which would then lead to your core offer (an online programme, or workshop, or whatever it is that you do).

You could also plan for a couple of webinars on the subject of public speaking and offer your core service with some additional bonuses. A great way to introduce new people to your business is to make a *bring a friend* offer (two for the price of one) to a VIP event (at the end of your 12 months maybe?) – where you then market your exclusive high-end offer.

Do you see how it all links together? By focusing on just one thing, public speaking and presenting with confidence, and by being clear on your core offer, you can be flexible with the other parts of your marketing and adjust them as necessary. Even if you are marketing offline and don't have the benefit of advanced analytics, you always have the end in mind.

Social media

As we've already discussed, you may not yet believe that you're in a position to decide which social media platform will work best for you, so include in your 30-day plan exactly which ones you will use for analysis and then move on.

Also come up with weekly topics/themes for your blogs, emails and other content, and include them on your plan so that you don't spend valuable time wracking your brains for inspiration (this is where online surveys and polls asking your audience what they want can be very useful).

Although it's important to structure your marketing, now and again you may find yourself having a flash of inspiration after a conversation with a client, and then decide to change the topic or theme for the week. Your daily activities will never be set in stone, so allow yourself to be creative whilst keeping an eye on the overall goals.

One of the questions I asked you at the beginning of this chapter was to decide how much time you wanted to spend marketing your business. Well of course that is going to depend a lot on whether you are combining online and offline, or if you are purely focusing on building your business via social media platforms.

If you are just starting out and have a limited number of clients then you are going to have more time for your marketing. But in a few months from now you could have so many clients that your time spent marketing has decreased significantly. No one size fits all, and you'll soon find out how much you can achieve in the time available to you.

A few words of caution. Never stop answering those comments on social media, and remain consistent with when you post your content. Don't drop the ball or your clients will drop you.

Remember to go and download the copies of my 90- and 30-day plans to get you started, and to revise all your plans on a monthly basis. **http://bit.ly/SIY_The_Downloads**

Other marketing opportunities

Here are just a few more ideas about how you could be promoting your products and services, as well as encouraging people to connect with you on social media and/or visit your website.

Firstly, make sure that your email signature includes links to all your social media profiles.

Secondly, include a link to your freebie or conversion tool somewhere in your email signature so that every single person you write to sees it. You never know who's watching!

Thirdly, and this works best if you're already using an email programme such as Mailchimp, use the bottom of the email to promote your other products, for example a VIP Breakthrough Session, or your new bestseller, or an upcoming webinar or other event.

It's such an easy thing to do, and the results can be astonishing. If you're using graphics just be careful of their size because if they're too big then your email will take a long time to load, and if it takes a long time to load ... well you already know what happens.

Summary

You have done the groundwork to create a marketing plan that will help you stand out way above your competition. It's a process, and you will change your mind about what's good and what isn't many times. Remember to pay attention to how you feel about your activities, and continue taking action.

Chapter 14 ~ Personal Branding and Your Business

"If I lost control of the business I'd lose myself–or at least the ability to be myself. Owning myself is a way to be myself." - Oprah Winfrey

This is it! Enter you stage right.

Theory is great, but putting a plan into action can sometimes seem like too big a hurdle, usually because somewhere at the back of your head you can still hear that little voice telling you that you can't do it.

There is a shocking statistic that 93 per cent of coaches who train and qualify fail to make it into the business world. That number is similar across all business sectors. Many people keep on looking for the next course or qualification because they don't think they're good enough. What a waste.

At this moment you are perfectly fabulous. At this moment you are good enough. At this moment you have everything it takes to succeed – if you want to.

One of the questions I am frequently asked is 'why is my personal brand important to my business', and the easy answer is that *you are* your business. Can you imagine going to a pet shop and being served by someone who disliked animals? Or working with a parenting coach who didn't like children?

I have selected three, short case studies so that you can see how your personal brand can influence your business success. Whilst my clients have given me permission to use their experiences as examples to help you, confidentiality is paramount to the work I do, and their names have been changed to protect their identity and business.

Keeping up appearances

Jenny and Jamie approached me when they discovered that their lives had become stressful, that they didn't have as much time as they would like to dedicate to their children let alone to each other, and that they were struggling to pay the bills.

In addition to running a small farm, they had a shop that sold vegetables, honey and other products from their bees. Jamie travelled to various markets throughout the week to sell their farm produce, and Jenny stayed at home to do everything else. They were both exhausted and very worried about the future, but Jenny and Jamie were committed to finding solutions.

Re-aligning with who you really are requires that you put aside all judgements and accusations, and before looking at the mechanics of Jenny's and Jamie's work, we explored their personal brands by clarifying their values, finding out what was important to them as individuals and why, and what they really enjoyed doing.

It quickly became clear that whilst Jamie loved spending time in the fresh air and looking after his bees, marketing and numbers were not his thing. He also discovered that he felt bad about not doing a lot of the farm work, work that he believed he *should* be doing, such as cutting the grass in the huge fields. He just didn't want to do it and was grumpy with himself.

Jenny was ready to drop. She was tired of being responsible for everything at home and the farm shop, and wanted to be able to have not only more quality time with her family, but also to follow her passion around natural remedies, something that had been on the back-burner for years.

We drilled down the activities that they both enjoyed in their current set up so that they could then see which gaps needed filling because there is a common mis-conception amongst many entrepreneurs and small business owners, namely that you need to do everything yourself. If you're starting out you tell yourself that you must focus on making money, and that you can't spend any.

All too often though, the result is that you end up being miserable, and your creativity and enthusiasm drops through the floor, which gets you the result you were doing your best to avoid.

There is no shame in asking for help, and once Jenny and Jamie had analysed how much time they were spending on things they didn't enjoy, making the decision to get support was very easy.

The next issue they faced was, who could they trust to run the farm shop, cut the grass in the huge fields, and clean the house. Using the same process that I have taught you about how to identify your five-start client, we created some very simple job descriptions that included the characteristics of the people they would want to work with.

That exercise helped them to expand their team in the confidence that they could still maintain the business image of family, warmth and a love of nature.

With the biggest problems out of the way, we then started on branding their business, bringing it into alignment with Jenny's and Jamie's core values, and building those values into their new logo, and then website.

Their transformation followed the steps that you have taken throughout this book. It didn't happen quickly by any means, in fact it took the best part of six months for Jenny and Jamie to re-prioritise and re-organise their lives. And for a short time they both took on part-time jobs to release the financial pressure they were feeling.

But the wonderful result is that now they are both more relaxed, they have more time for each other and for their children, and they know with certainty that they can make their business profitable without running themselves into the ground.

The lesson here was that both Jenny and Jamie had wanted their business to grow, yet neither of them had questioned whether the other partner was in agreement with what was involved (responsibilities). It also emerged that neither of them had wanted to admit that they felt out of their depth.

Their attention was concentrated on what was happening around them – outward looking – instead of questioning how they *felt* about the direction that the business was going in – inward looking.

You are the CEO of you, regardless of whether you're a solopreneur or manager of many. If you're clear on your values and why you do what you do, you and others will be clear on your personal brand, and you'll save yourself a lot of heartache further down the line.

Lipstick, powder and paint

Zoe was the owner of a small shop selling cosmetics and wanted to grow her team to be able to provide treatments such as manicures and pedicures. Up until we met, she and her employees had covered all the tasks together and she was at the point of wanting to split up everyone's duties to be able to increase marketing activities, before taking on additional staff.

When Zoe came to me she was frustrated because she had given one of her employees the task of going to trade fairs and exhibitions, and her colleague was resisting. She felt as though her authority was being called into question, and that her team should do as she asked.

As we began working through the process of aligning her personal brand with her business, Zoe discovered that she had moved from being a team member to a team leader, and that the two roles were very different. Her brand had evolved from being the smiley colleague who happened to work at the shop, to the person in charge and the face of the business for the outside world.

We worked on a strategy to help Zoe better present herself with authority, and to manage her team effectively without causing ill-feeling. And because Zoe cared deeply about her colleagues, I worked with them individually to help them establish their strengths and agree on their contribution.

It emerged that the person who had been asked to work on external marketing was petrified of meeting new people. She was very happy to work on social media and organise advertising from her desk but selling to others sent her into a panic. Because the team had previously done everything together, Zoe wasn't aware of her colleague's concerns, and as soon as the issue came to light, duties were re-arranged accordingly.

The result was that Zoe's team worked more effectively than ever before, so that when the new staff came on board, they were welcomed into an environment where everyone was the authority for their own duties. By making her staff accountable for their input and helping them to align to their values and strengths, Zoe also positioned herself as a leader that her team could respect, and from whom they could take instruction without disagreement.

This scenario is very common when managing a team. When a business is small it's easy to adopt an 'all hands on deck' approach. The working relationships are strong because you all have to depend on each other, and colleagues become friends.

If you then want to change the team set up and you assert your authority as boss, some of your colleagues may feel threatened. One day you're their friend, and the next you're telling them what to do. Your personal brand has changed.

As was the case with Zoe, you will already know that your personal brand is changing by how you feel inside, and it's up to you to manage that change with what's happening around you. It requires self-reflection and honesty, and you must be clear on the role that you want and why it's important to you. After that, everything gets easier.

From corporate to charity

My final case study is one of my favourite success stories because the situation was extreme and when it happened, the transformation changed my client's life beyond recognition.

Lisa was a lawyer who had been working as a consultant in a corporate environment for several years, and whilst she had excellent qualifications and her fees paid the bills, she came to me because she wanted to position herself as an expert in family law.

When we first met she had begun to apply to jobs in large organisations because she couldn't see any other way to do what she loved the most.

As with every other client, I took Lisa through all the exercises included in this book. She was passionate about helping others, and having come from a poor background, she also wanted to have a healthy income. Yet this was one of many contradictions that Lisa discovered about herself, believing that only dishonest and corrupt people had lots of money.

Another belief that we worked through was that she had to do what her parents expected her to because they had paid for her education and she wanted to be a dutiful daughter.

At times it felt as though Lisa's confidence in her abilities was rock-bottom, and that everything she had done all her life had been to please others. She discovered that she had been holding herself back from success for fear of being judged by her family, and being accused of thinking that she was better than the rest of them.

As the weeks went by she was less and less clear about who she was and what she wanted to do because very little of what she learned through our work didn't match the personal brand of the corporate lawyer/consultant she had given herself.

After nine weeks of releasing limiting beliefs and contradictions, we did something called the *rocking chair test*, the ultimate method of working backwards from your goals.

Activity: The Rocking Chair Test

Find some quiet time to close your eyes and imagine that you're celebrating your 90th Birthday with all your family and friends.

You're sitting in your rocking chair enjoying the festivities, and one of the guests approaches you.

They sit on the floor next to you and ask you to tell them what was the best thing that ever happened in your life, or maybe what you were most proud of. What do you say?

Your answer to that question could provide you with new inspiration – and so it was with Lisa.

The next time we met she was a different person. She was shining with happiness. Lisa told me that as she was doing the rocking chair test she saw lots of layers fall away in her mind.

She had seen herself dressed in desert clothing working with women and children and that she now knew that she wanted to provide legal advice to charities in Africa.

She talked so fast about her plans that it was hard to keep up. I have never seen such enthusiasm and desire, and Lisa said that a huge weight had been lifted from her life. Within two weeks she had packed up and gone to make her new dream a reality.

We're still in touch and she is one of the happiest people I know.

Summary

Aligning your personal brand with your work can be *the* difference between happiness and misery, success and failure, wealth and lack. Although it may take you longer than you would like, you owe it to yourself to find out what you value and what you love to do. When you are comfortable being authentic, magical things happen.

Onwards.

Chapter 15 ~ Preparing Your First Business Pitch or Presentation

"A few mistakes do not a fiasco make. Professionals throw them off casually but file them away to reinvent as an endearing anecdote in later presentations.
Make them part of the performance!
Put them behind you and keep going whatever happens." –
Ruth Bonetti

How long do you usually spend preparing for a business meeting or networking event? Do you have a quick look at the company's website or check out your contact person's profile on LinkedIn?

Would your preparation time be longer if you knew that your next cup of coffee or presentation had the power to change your business forever?

One of the things that is going to make you stand out from everyone else, especially when it comes to pitching for new business, is the fact that you will have taken the time to really understand your potential client, what they need, and how you can deliver on their expectations.

You will know by now that one of the most business-relevant quotes of all time is "begin with the end in mind" from the late Stephen Covey, author of "The Seven Habits of Highly Effective People". When you first clarify your goal, you know where you're going and so have a much better chance of getting there.

Being clear on your desired outcome in advance of every single cup of coffee, informal meeting, business presentation or marketing pitch will increase your chances of success. And that's a promise.

Be a private investigator (part 2)

In Chapter 7 you researched your clients from your personal perspective ie., matching your values with the types of people you wanted to work with. You're going to do it again here so that you understand what your potential client *will want from you*.

Every time you meet with new clients (and assuming you already know that you want to work with them), regardless of the setting or the purpose of your conversation, you must research them rigorously. Understanding who they are and what is important to them is going to work in your favour when it comes to building rapport and empathy. As you already know, their website or other online (social media) presence is the easiest place to start.

Begin by looking at the type of language and expressions they use.

No-one expects you to change the way that you speak, but the results from your research are going to help you decide on the language, key words and phrases you use when you're talking to a potential client.

For example, *you* may talk about having clients, but if you're working with a fitness club, *they* are going to be talking about members, and if you're talking to a retailer they'll use the word customer or consumer, and if you're talking to someone in the medical profession they may talk about patients.

Look at the photographs they have posted online. If you see pictures of people dressed in formal business attire, you aren't going to want to turn up in jeans and a t-shirt with sparkly flip-flops. You're already clear on the image that *you* want to promote, and now you simply need to adapt that image to match (to the extent possible) the style of your client.

If you see that the differences are too big, don't work with them! Which values are important to them? Do you get the impression that they place greater focus on their customers or their products, or their staff? How long has the company been in business and how big is it? Can you find out what their annual turnover is? Have they published any press releases on new offers? Does the company contribute to a charity?

If they have a social media presence, how much interaction is there? Which platforms do they use? How regularly do they post? What sort of content are they sharing?

If you were the business owner or CEO of the company in question, what would be important to you? Do you see any gaps or inconsistencies in their mission statement?

There are many more questions that you could be asking yourself to research your potential client, and you may find it useful to create your own checklist for every meeting so that you don't forget anything important.

Even if you have met these people before, check their website again and see whether they have started any new projects, or added to their blog, or completely changed their branding.

By making sure that you are as up to date on their activities as you can be, you will be three steps ahead of the competition.

Presentation structure

You know that you are the answer to all their problems, but the people to whom you are presenting don't, at least not yet, and you need to come up with some ideas to convince them that you are their only choice.

You must connect with your audience at an emotional level, and your presentation needs to tell a story. There are a couple of ways that you can do this, depending on what you have been asked to talk about.

You already have a substantial personal branding content library full of examples demonstrating how brilliantly you use your skills to get results. Put yourself in the shoes of your (potential) client. What do they want to hear?

If you have been invited to introduce yourself as a prospective business partner ie., you are going to be marketing yourself and your business, you can easily use the 5 C's system that I gave you in Chapter 8 and describe what you do using examples of your success with previous clients (context, crisis, course of action, challenges, celebration).

If you have been asked to pitch for a contract requiring a solution to a specific problem, for example the company in question is looking for a branding coach to help them strengthen their image, or an HR consultant to help them manage their next recruitment drive, you will take a more detailed approach.

There is magic in the power of threes and you should use the presentation to highlight the three skills you possess that you believe to be most important in solving the client's problem(s). This is a time proven structure that is easy to prepare for and easy for those watching to understand.

1.   Begin with a statistic related to the problem, for example "despite companies investing millions on recruitment, staff engagement statistics have remained at the gloomy level of just 15 per cent for almost 20 years."

2.   Set out what you are going to tell your audience, for example "I would like to share with you three things that can transform the way you recruit new staff – how to create job advertisements that are going to attract your ideal employees at a greatly reduced cost, how to build engagement from the day that your new colleague walks through the door, and how to maintain high levels of performance and productivity, even when the numbers don't look so good."

3.   You then introduce yourself and your company with the profile/elevator pitch that you created in Chapter 9.

4.   Your next step is to begin with the first problem you spoke about and to use relevant examples of your previous successes to demonstrate your first skill. Use the 5 Cs and follow this process for the next two problems/solutions/skills.

5. Conclude by summarising what you have just told your audience and ask them if they have any questions.

6. Agree on the next steps, for example are they going to call you in a week, or do they require more information, or do they want written references from other clients? Don't leave until a course of action is decided upon, and paraphrase back to your audience to ensure that you have understood them correctly.

7. Always send an email thanking those concerned for the opportunity to present/pitch.

Be authentic. Be sincere. Be you.

Trust that if you and your potential client are the perfect match then you are going to be working together.

It really is that simple.

Follow a structure and not a script, because if you attempt to create a narrative for yourself whereby you then have to memorise every single word of what you have written, at the first sign of nervousness you could forget a sentence and mess up the whole thing.

Creating a structure such as that above means that you only have to remember which step comes next, and as you become more comfortable with storytelling using the information you have in your personal branding content library, you will find that your presentations flow beautifully.

To Powerpoint or not

Hmmm. This is a tricky one because from my experience everyone has a different idea of what constitutes a great presentation. There is one way to get an answer to this question though, and that is to check in advance of your meeting what your prospective client wants.

You will anyway need to clarify how long the presentation should last, whether it should include time for questions and answers, how many people will be attending and their level of seniority, *and* what type of equipment is available.

Most companies have some sort of equipment that you can use and if it's a smaller and more informal meeting, you will be able to get away with having a few select slides to show on your laptop.

However, as a failsafe I have an entire kit at home consisting of a projector, a USB-operated slide clicker to move through the presentation without having to go back to my laptop, adaptor cables for my laptop so that I can plug it in anywhere, a Bose speaker that connects to my laptop via Bluetooth so that I can have music playing when people arrive if appropriate, a flipchart and extra paper, notebooks to hand out, and branded pens. Just saying.

Keep your presentation simple. If there are too many flashing animations and spinning colours you will end up with a frustrated audience.

- *Do* include pictures around which you can tell your story (your elevator pitch).

- *Do* include pictures around which you can describe your success stories, and which portray companies similar to the one you are talking to (although be wary of including pictures and/or stories about competitors).

- *Do* include the name of your company together with the copyright symbol at the bottom of each of the slides (you can never be too careful).

- *Do* include graphs to present financial information (much easier to interpret than lots of written numbers).

- *Do* practise your presentation so that you're not having to constantly look at notes – remember that any time you pitch you will be influencing your future success. If you're nervous and don't believe you can remember everything, print off the slides (six or nine to a page) and write one or two bullet points next to each.

- *Don't* include slides with lines and lines of text which you just then read off. If all the information is already on screen, your audience doesn't need you.

- *Don't* give your audience a copy of your presentation unless they specifically ask for it (even then, never in advance because you could kill their interest).

Handouts

As mentioned above, don't give your audience copies of your presentation (if you have one) in advance, and don't give them folders containing testimonials from other clients or other information that could distract them whilst you are speaking.

What can be very useful however is to have something to distribute after you have finished.

You may not be able to go into as much detail as you would like to on some topics during your presentation and therefore a document containing additional statistics, charts and graphics – anything that strengthens your case – will not only be useful for your audience but will also demonstrate that you have clearly taken the time to consider their needs.

All your handouts should include your business branding, and at the end of the document include your contact details, and if you feel comfortable doing so, your social media sites.

Summary

Research your audience and focus your presentation on what *they* need to hear. Use their key words and phrases in your presentation to strengthen your connection with them and work from a structure, not a narrative.

Check what your audience is expecting from you well in advance of your meeting, and confirm the availability of equipment.

Chapter 16 ~ Keeping Your Personal Brand Steady

"You only grow by coming to the end of something and by beginning something else." –
John Irving

Whoooossshhh!   Do you see the difference in yourself since you started this book?

It's time for you to get out there and show the world what you've got, and I have given you the tools that you need to make sure that others remember you for the right reasons every time.

You're going to keep growing, both personally and professionally, and that means that your brand will evolve with you because you're human, and tomorrow you will be a different person than you were yesterday or today.

So how do you keep your personal brand steady? The answer to that question is self-awareness. You need to check in with yourself on a regular basis. You should already be aware of how your marketing is going by revising your planning documents every 30 days, and your bank balance is also going to be an indicator of your material success.

But you also need to be aware of how you feel. As I've mentioned many times, if your work is beginning to feel as though you're walking through thick mud, there is no point in continuing in the hope that things will get better. There's a big difference between being tired because you've over-stretched yourself and being fed-up because what you're no longer doing what excites you.

Listen to your body. Listen to your thoughts. Listen to your feelings. Follow your gut instincts and follow your intuition. I'm not talking about being impulsive and completely changing direction, I'm asking you to be honest with yourself when things don't feel great.

Go back to your what and your why

Procrastination is one of the greatest enemies of a solopreneur. We get so caught up in the minutiae of creating fabulous content and programmes and graphics that we put off picking up the telephone to talk to a client, or we decide to not go to a networking event because we've been working so hard that we believe we deserve an afternoon or evening off.

Of course you deserve time off, but if you continue to reason with yourself about why you shouldn't be taking decisive, outcome-oriented action to build your brand and your business, eventually you will turn the tables on yourself and say that nothing is working, and if it isn't working it must mean that you're no good at what you do, that you're a complete failure, and that therefore you are not going to bother any more.

As soon as you feel yourself slipping, go back to your *what* and your *why*. Go back to the work you did at the beginning of this book and rediscover what inspired and motivated you to start this journey. Maybe you need to break your goals down even further, maybe you need to take things more slowly, maybe you need to delegate some of the tasks that you don't enjoy.

Find your community

Can you imagine if you had arrived on the planet and your parents had told you that you were responsible for teaching yourself how to eat, dress yourself, tie your shoelaces, read and write...? You cannot build your personal brand and business in isolation, it's just impossible.

I wouldn't be here today without the support of some fabulous mentors and coaches from whom I learned so much, including the fact that the only person holding you back from stardom and success is the one looking back at you from the mirror in your bathroom.

When you're searching for groups online to do your networking, make sure that there is at least one where you can learn new things.

When you're choosing which networking events to go to, make sure that you include one or two where you are going to meet solopreneurs just like you.

Be supportive and allow yourself to be supported. Become part of a community where you have a sense of belonging.

Evolution

Do yourself a favour and commit to taking time every month to look at your marketing strategy and plans. As you're reading through the analytics and insights, *listen* to what you're *feeling*. I promise you, your gut instinct, intuition or whatever else you want to call it is going to be your most reliable source of feedback when it comes to developing your personal brand and your business.

You will change and *your business* will change. Remember that it's ok to change. You are the boss of you, you are in charge of your business, so stay aligned and do what you *feel* is right.

There is no shame in taking a different course or recreating your entire personal brand if that's where you find yourself heading. It's not a demonstration of failure, it's simply evidence that you are learning more about what you love to do and taking ownership for your future. Do what's best for you, and everything else will fall into place.

Align. Release. Trust. Transform. Thrive.

Epilogue – Would Madam Prefer Veuve Clicquot or Taittinger?

I have loved writing this book and my passion and desire for you to succeed has been my 'why'. You have a gift for others in the form of your personal brand and your business, and you owe it to yourself and others to acknowledge it and share it. Allow yourself to be fabulous and celebrate every step of your journey.

And remember to come and connect with me online so that I can keep cheering you on.

Mine's an ice-cold glass of pink Veuve Clicquot, thank you. What's yours?

Much love
Gwyneth xx

ACKNOWLEDGEMENTS

The list of people to whom thanks are owed is long, but there are a few to whom I would specifically like to express my gratitude.

My entire family far and wide has provided hours of encouragement in various forms, as have some very special friends – Angela, Ardita, Gabi, Hilda, Katherine and Vlora. Even though there were times when each of you didn't have a clue what I was talking about, you never suggested that I give up.

I also couldn't have completed this book without the support of some extraordinary coaches and mentors in the form of Carol and David Standing (Accordant Partners), Alison Jones (Book Coach) and Veronica Pullen (the Social Marketing Queen).

Norik Uka is the clever photographer who understood my ideas and provided the fabulous photograph for the book cover, and it was the wonderful Sarah Smith who put the photograph and text together to make the book cover beautiful. Antonia Maxwell provided constructive feedback on my writing style in the nicest way possible.

And finally, even though she can't read, I'm going to say thank you to Twinkle, the Kosovo street dog who adopted me 10 years ago and who now lives with me on my hill in Austria, who never questions who she is, who never changes her behavior to be a different type of dog, who trusts that she will always be loved (and fed) despite her unhappy start in life, and who has sat faithfully by my side for so many hours as I have looked for the words that you read here.

BIBLIOGRAPHY

Books

Assaraf, J. (2007) "Having it all"

Allen, D. (2015) "Getting Things Done: The Art of Stress Free Productivity"

Babcock, L. and Laschever, S. (2003) "Women Don't Ask: Negotiation and the Gender Divide"

Cialdini, R. B. (2009) "Influence"

Covey, S. (2004) "The 7 Habits of Highly Effective People: Powerful Lessons in Personal Change"

Goleman, D. (2005) 'Emotional Intelligence: Why It Can Matter More Than IQ'

Hendricks, G. PhD (2009) "The Big Leap: Conquer Your Hidden Fear and Take Life to the Next Level"

Websites

Affirmations - www.johnassaraf.com/law-of-attraction/making-your-affirmations-more-powerful
Accessed 2 November 2017

Barclays report - 'Untapped Unicorns: scaling up female entrepreneurship', https://www.home.barclays/news/2017/03/untapped-unicorns--scaling-up-female-entrepreneurship.html
Accessed 17 July 2017

Ego - www.en.oxforddictionaries.com/definition/ego
Accessed 9 August 2017

Emotional Intelligence – www.histoiredintuition.com/2014/02/12/emotional-intelligence-intuitive-intelligence-end-iq-hegemony/).
Accessed 19 August 2017

Erskine,Ryan - 22 Statistics that Prove the Value of Personal Branding',
www.ryanerskine.com/blog/22-statistics-that-prove-the-value-of-personal-branding

Facebook statistics - www.smartinsights.com/social-media-marketing/social-media-strategy/new-global-social-media-research/
Accessed 19 August 2017

Google - www.learndigital.withgoogle.com/digitalgarage/
Accessed 23 September 2017

Hooponopono - www.hoomanaspamaui.com/meaning-of-hooponopono/
Accessed 12 August 2017

Lewin's Change Management Model -
www.mindtools.com/pages/article/newPPM_94.htm).
Accessed 15 August 2017

LinkedIn statistics www.expandedramblings.com
Accessed19 August 2017

Meditation - www.deepakchopra.com
Accessed 12 August 2017

Pinterest statistics - www.blog.hootsuite.com/pinterest-statistics-for-business/
Accessed 23 September 2017

Reticular Activating System -
www.joecasanova.com/2015/12/16/reticularactivatingsystem/
Accessed 7 October 2017

Social Media Statistics
www.hootsuite.com Accessed 19 August 2017
www.statista.com Accessed 19 March 2018
www.expandedramblings.com Accessed 19 March 2018

Resources

Links to all **BONUS DOWNLOADS**: http://bit.ly/SIY_The_Downloads

Jane Jackson, EFT (tapping) Practitioner: www.jane-jackson.co.uk

Victoria Lochhead, Personal Stylist: www.frankieandruby.co.uk

Veronica Pullen, Social Marketing Queen: www.veronicapullen.co.uk

Carol Standing, Create Sales on a Daily Basis:
www.accordantpartners.co.uk

Sarah Smith (book cover) and Antonia Maxwell (copy editor) can both be found at www.reedsy.com

Graphics and images: www.canva.com

Social media marketing scheduling: www.hootsuite.com

WIX websites: www.wix.com

ABOUT THE AUTHOR

Gwyneth is a Personal Branding Strategist and Professional Development Coach, Author and Speaker.

Born in England, she spent 25 years working throughout Europe and the Balkans, building and managing multi-cultural teams. After gaining her MBA and qualifying as a coach, she established her own consultancy based on her understanding and experience of complex workplace challenges.

She now provides specialist consultancy services, online training, and workshops all over the world to help people working in an international business environment discover their personal brand and transform the way that they communicate with their colleagues, and market and promote themselves.

Gwyneth lives and works from her home on a hill in Upper Austria and spends her free time gardening. She also loves getting up at the crack of dawn to walk her dogs in the surrounding forest.

Visit www.feelgoodcoachingandconsulting.com if you would like to get in touch or subscribe to the Feelgood Coaching and Consulting YouTube Channel for Gwyneth's Fabulous Feelgood Friday vlog.